Minimalists

by K. Robert Schwarz

To my parents, Boris and Patricia Schwarz, who started my life in music

Phaidon Press Limited
Regent's Wharf
All Saints Street
London N1 9PA

First published 1996
© 1996 Phaidon Press Limited

ISBN 0 7148 3381 9

A CIP catalogue record for this book is available from the British Library

Printed in Singapore

Frontispiece, the pioneer of musical minimalism in a frontier pose: La Monte Young, Berlin, 1992

Contents

Acknowledgements

Many do not consider minimalism to be an entirely respectable field of academic pursuit, and so I must thank two open-minded professors – H. Wiley Hitchcock at the City University of New York and Austin B. Caswell at Indiana University – who encouraged and supported the research I did while still in university. There has been relatively little scholarly investigation of minimalism, but an exception is the superb work of Edward Strickland (*Minimalism: Origins* and *American Composers: Dialogues on Contemporary Music*), to which I am indebted.

Since much of the quoted material included here comes from interviews I conducted, I must particularly thank those composers – John Adams, Steve Reich, Terry Riley, and La Monte Young – who agreed to be cross-examined for this volume. I should also thank those composers – Louis Andriessen, Philip Glass, Meredith Monk and Michael Nyman – who were interviewed at other times for various purposes. And I must acknowledge the generosity of Dunvagen Music Publishers, which granted me permission to quote extensively from Glass's autobiography *Music by Philip Glass* (1987).

Finally, thanks are due to those who assisted me in assembling scores, tapes, CDs, and articles: Mary Lou Humphrey (G. Schirmer), Jim Keller (Dunvagen), Tina Pelikan (ECM), Steven Swartz (Boosey & Hawkes), Jed Wheeler (International Production Associates), and Carol Yaple (Nonesuch).

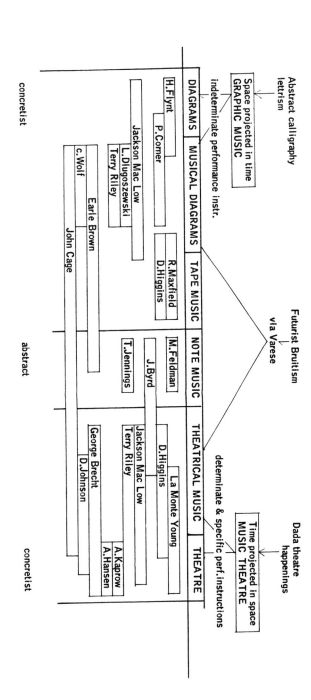

Space projected in time GRAPHIC MUSIC/Time projected in space MUSIC THEATRE by George Maciunas of the anarchical Fluxus group of artists and thinkers; this diagram from 1961 is in the Gilbert and Lila Silverman Collection.

Introduction: Minimalism Defined

No style of late twentieth-century music has provoked as much controversy as minimalism. To its supporters, its directness and accessibility restores the severed link between composer and audience. To its detractors, it is maddeningly simple-minded, no better than pop music masquerading as art. And to its creators, the term itself is burdened with pejorative connotations. It is no wonder that the two most famous minimalist composers, Steve Reich and Philip Glass, despise the word and reject its relevance to their present-day work.

But the public, it would seem, has had the last laugh. Despite three decades of unrelenting ridicule from mainstream composers and critics – who have coined such unflattering descriptions as 'going-nowhere music', 'needle-stuck-in-the-groove music', and 'wallpaper music' – minimalism has become an enormous commercial success. Glass and Reich produce best-selling recordings, receive prestigious commissions, and perform to sold-out houses. And their audience is unprecedented in the world of twentieth-century concert music, not only for its size, but for its diversity – an improbable blend of classical, pop, and world-music fans.

What kind of music can incite simultaneously such scorn and such acclaim? Just what exactly is minimalism?

Like Impressionism, the term minimalism was borrowed from the visual arts. And, again like Impressionism, it was initially used with derision. American painters such as Frank Stella and Robert Rauschenberg, who reduced their canvases to solid swaths of black or white, and sculptors such as Richard Serra and Donald Judd, who created huge, uninflected cubes or arcs, had all had been mocked as 'minimalists'. With understandable annoyance and embarrassment, the English composer and critic Michael Nyman admits to being the culprit responsible for transferring the word to music. 'When I introduced it to music in 1968, it was a valid art-historical term,' he said in 1991. 'And without thinking about it too much, it seemed that there was a musical parallel. That was twenty-three years ago, and one would think that the public's perception of the music would have changed. But we're all still hung with this albatross, which is used simply as a way of packaging something.'

Still, the albatross wouldn't have survived for so long if it did not have a certain validity. La Monte Young, a composer who is often revered as the grand-daddy of minimalism, defines the style succinctly and elegantly: 'That which is created with a minimum of means.' Minimalist music is based on the notion of reduction, the paring down to a minimum of the materials that a composer will use in a given work. In the classic minimalist compositions of the 1960s, practically every musical element – harmony, rhythm, dynamics, instrumentation – remains fixed for the duration of the work, or changes only very slowly. And the chief structural technique is unceasing repetition, exhilarating to some, mind-numbing to others.

In traditional Western classical music, repetition is used within the context of a dramatic, directionalized form. (Think, for instance, of the development section of a symphony, where the repetition of motivic fragments enables the movement to build to a frenzy of excitement.) But in minimalism, repetition is used to create what Glass has called 'intentionless music', which replaces goal-oriented directionality with absolute stasis. Like so much non-Western music, minimalist pieces do not drive toward climaxes, do not build up patterns of tension and release, and do not provide emotional catharses. They demand a new kind of listening, one lacking in 'traditional concepts of recollection and anticipation', as Glass has put it. In minimalism, you will not find the contrasts – loud and soft, fast and slow, bombastic or lyrical – that are the substance of Western classical music. In fact, minimalism challenges our perception of time itself, since the music changes almost imperceptibly over minutes or even hours.

It is not surprising, therefore, that minimalism owes as much to non-Western traditions as to Western classical music. The four path-breaking American minimalists – La Monte Young, Terry Riley, Reich, and Glass – all immersed themselves in non-Western music, whether Indian raga, Balinese gamelan, or West African drumming. Although they didn't try to imitate the sound of non-Western music, they certainly embraced its contemplative, time-suspending qualities. In that respect they were very much a product of the 1960s – a decade when the Beatles brought elements of Indian music into rock, and

when Eastern philosophy, meditation, and the drug-induced perceptual alterations of psychedelia went hand in hand.

But minimalism, which was born in the USA, could never have
developed without a strong infusion of American popular culture. The
harmonic simplicity, steady pulse and rhythmic drive of jazz and rock-
and-roll had an incalculable impact on the pioneering minimalists,
who grew up listening to popular music and playing in bands.
Eventually, in true pop-music fashion, all four composers created (and
performed in) their own ensembles. Playing in venues more associated
with rock than with classical music, groups like the Philip Glass
Ensemble or Steve Reich and Musicians toured the globe. Faced with
the blasting volume, pounding beat, and electronic instrumentation
of Glass's ensemble, it is no wonder that rock fans flocked in droves –
and academics went running in the other direction.

Yet it would be wrong only to emphasize minimalism's roots
outside of Western classical music. The contemplative quality of
Gregorian chant, the stasis of medieval organum, the repetitive,
motoric rhythms of Baroque music – all share certain qualities with
twentieth-century minimalism. And there are more recent musical
precedents in the West, such as the burbling, three-minute-long, E
flat major chord that opens Wagner's *Das Rheingold*, the relentlessly
repeated melody of Ravel's *Boléro*, or the works of Erik Satie (especially his infamous *Vexations*, which demands that a single musical
phrase be repeated 840 times).

Revolutions in the arts are typically the result of a profound reaction against the conventions of a preceding generation, and minimalism is no exception. When Young, Riley, Reich and Glass were music
students in the late 1950s, there were two alternative paths through the
musical avant garde. One, following from the twelve-note technique
of Arnold Schoenberg and Anton Webern, was the path of serialism –
a dogmatic, mathematical, super-rational approach to composition
that resulted in atonal works of daunting complexity. Serial music, as
refined by the American composer Milton Babbitt, was so hair-rais-
ingly difficult that only the privileged few could understand it. Yet it
became the enshrined academic manner – the style that a young
composer had to work in if he were to be taken seriously.

The other (and far less respectable) path was indeterminacy,
the 'chance music' created by John Cage and his disciples. Cage,

himself under the influence of Eastern philosophy, proposed a Zen-like acceptance of all the sounds around us as viable sources of music. The results could be messy and shocking, closer to theatrical 'happenings' than conventionally musical sounds. But Cage's philosophy represented a genuine sonic liberation that would have immense consequences.

The minimalists began their careers by forcefully rejecting both serialism and indeterminacy – one for its needless complexity, the other for its chaotic freedom. Yet in truth they owed a debt to both. The music of Webern, often minimal in length and nearly inaudible in dynamics, included static elements that Young, especially, found inspiring. And it could be argued that Cage, as far back as 1952, had already composed the ultimate minimalist work. His *4'33"*, the title of which refers to its length, is a silent piece in which no sounds are specified by the composer. The sounds of the environment – including, perhaps, the outraged shrieks of the audience – comprise the music.

When you start a revolution, you are inclined to argue the most extreme position first, and only later move toward compromise. And the minimalists were no exception. In spurning both Babbitt and Cage, they were assured of condemnation by both academia and the avant garde. By re-embracing the primal forces of clear tonality and steady pulse, which both the serialists and the Cageians had declared dead, they turned that condemnation into outright ridicule.

The minimalists, for their part, proposed a music that was every bit as radical as what they were rejecting. Reich's terse and strident essay of 1968, 'Music as a Gradual Process', today reads like no less than a political manifesto. Although it was meant to apply only to his own music, it offers insights into the minimalist aesthetic as a whole.

Reich emphasized that the structure of the music – what he calls the 'musical process' – must be audible to the listener. To ensure that audibility, the process must unfold very systematically and very slowly. 'I am interested in perceptible processes,' he wrote. 'I want to be able to hear the processes happening throughout the sounding music. To facilitate closely detailed listening, a musical process should happen extremely gradually ... so slowly that listening to it resembles watching the minute hand on a watch – you can perceive it moving after you stay with it a little while.'

Clearly Reich was repudiating the hidden, inaudible structural devices of both serialism and indeterminacy. Just as clearly, he was proposing (and already composing) a music that had no literal precedent in the West. If processes were to unfold as gradually as he sought, the music would have to occupy vast expanses of time. And if those processes were to remain perceptible, the music would demand an extraordinary amount of what at first might sound like unvarnished repetition. Only after several minutes of close listening – the aural equivalent of following the watch's minute hand – would the transformations wrought by the process become evident.

To a listener brought up on the passion and climactic sweep of Beethoven and Tchaikovsky, this new minimalist music must have seemed like the sonic equivalent of Chinese water-torture. But to listeners weaned on the kinetic repetitions of jazz and rock, or the lengthy time-frames of non-Western music, it was surprisingly accessible. In fact, minimalist works can have the quality of a slowly unfolding, ecstatic ritual, and if you submit yourself to that ritual the result can be exhilarating. 'My own feeling is that if people aren't carried away to heaven I'm failing,' said Young in 1966. 'Obviously music should put all within listening range into a state of ecstasy,' said Reich in 1969. When before had twentieth-century classical music, previously so dour and alienating, spoken in such user-friendly terms?

Minimalist music, in its purest and most rigorous form, was first composed by Young in the late 1950s and Riley in the early 1960s. (Reich and Glass did not come onto the scene until the mid- and late 1960s, respectively.) By the mid-1970s, Reich and Glass were the commercial hub of the movement, and they had already begun to turn away from the reductive extremes of their earlier work. In fact by the early 1980s it made little sense to speak of either composer as a 'minimalist'. Yet they continue to be saddled with the label, however inappropriate.

And they continue to be saddled with each other as well. The minimalist Fab Four, as they have jokingly been dubbed by the historian Edward Strickland, have resented a tendency to lump them together; they have rightly observed that their musical styles are extremely different. Meanwhile, their varying degree of commercial success has bred competitiveness among the Fab Four and reduced them to a disputatious, dysfunctional family. 'Even the Borgias look like a happy family by comparison', wrote the critic John Schaefer.

Still, before looking at the lives of the minimalists, it is worth noting that this family does have a certain amount in common. All four minimalists were born in America in the mid-1930s; all grew up enamoured of American popular music; all endured (and rejected) their European-oriented conservatory training; all tuned their minds to the sounds and rituals of Asia; and all, over time, became profoundly religious. Each found a unique path to the highly reductive and genuinely accessible music that we have come to call minimalism.

And what of the term itself? For better or worse, it has become universally accepted. Shorn of its original derisive implications, minimalism is better than the many other terms – trance music, hypnotic music, repetitive music – that have also been proposed. Besides, composers do not have the luxury of deciding how they will be labelled by history; all they can do is sit back and try to make peace with the result. As Reich has observed of the unfortunate '-isms' that plagued his predecessors: 'Debussy resented "Impressionism". Schoenberg preferred "pantonal" to "atonal" or "twelve-tone" or "Expressionist". Too bad for them.'

I

*Bring a bale of hay and a bucket of water onto
the stage for the piano to eat and drink. The
performer may then feed the piano or leave it to
eat by itself. If the former, the piece is over after
the piano has been fed. If the latter, it is over
after the piano eats or decides not to.*

La Monte Young's *Piano Piece
for David Tudor #1*

La Monte Young and Terry Riley

The wind howled across the Idaho plains and shook the very foundation of the tiny log cabin in which he slept. But the little boy, rather
than being frightened, was fascinated by the long, sustained roar.

> *I got this start lying in my bed in the log cabin, hearing the wind
> blow between the criss-crossed logs. The winds in the winter could
> be ferocious; there would be blizzards, and you couldn't see a hand
> in front of your face. I tried to come to terms with that at the age of two
> or three. It wasn't as if I could turn off the wind, like somebody would
> turn off the radio; when one of those storms came it went on as long as it
> was going to last. And I found it to be very profound and awesome.*

Obviously, La Monte Young's propensity for constant, unchanging
sounds was already established in his childhood. And what a childhood it was. Some American composers have had to invent a frontier
upbringing in order to add to the allure of their biographies. But for
Young, who was born on 14 October 1935 in the hamlet of Bern,
Idaho, the frontier was all he knew.

In 1935 Bern was a Mormon dairy community blessed with 149
hard-working and God-fearing citizens. Located in the Bear River
valley, nestled between the barren foothills of the Teton range, Bern
was surrounded by desolate, sagebrush-covered prairie and buffeted
relentlessly by the elements. La Monte's parents, Dennis and Ella
Young, have been described by their son as 'hillbillies'. Certainly they
were desperately poor. Dennis, a sheep-herder, lived with his family
in a two-room cabin along the shore of the Bear River.

Despite these humble beginnings, music played a significant role
in Young's childhood. His father and aunt encouraged him to join
them in singing cowboy songs, and he learned enough guitar by the
age of four to accompany them. In church, he participated when the
congregation sang hymns. When he was four his family allowed him
to tap-dance and sing at the Rich Theater in Montpelier, Idaho, the

region's largest town. There his grandparents lived, and he was able to experiment with their upright piano.

Still, it was less music itself than the sounds of the environment that impressed the boy. 'After I started being able to walk around I heard one of these telephone poles with the transformer on it, and I found that very fascinating to listen to,' Young recalled recently. Soon Dennis Young got a job at the Conoco oil-distribution plant in Montpelier, and he would take La Monte to work with him. 'Right next door to that plant – and I've gone back many times since to look at it and listen to it – is a little transformer station that somehow steps down the power for Montpelier. I used to like to stand next to that and listen to it.' He was intuitively drawn to the droning hum, even if he had no means of categorizing what he heard. 'I don't think I had a concept yet of sustained tones. It's just that I heard these sustained sounds coming out of the transformers and I was fascinated.'

In 1941, when rural America was still struggling to rouse itself from the Depression, the Young family hitchhiked to Los Angeles so Dennis could look for work. He found a job in a machine shop but the Youngs remained poor; La Monte remembers eating bread and milk for dinner. So the fact that Dennis purchased a saxophone for his son suggests that the boy demonstrated extraordinary musical talent.

The humble log cabin in Bern, Idaho, La Monte Young's birthplace

La Monte Young seated on his horse, in front of his family's farmhouse in American Fork, Utah, c. 1946-7

'When I was about seven years old, my father brought home an old silver saxophone, which was really practically grey,' Young said. 'Because my father was so authoritarian, I asked my mother if Dad might give me saxophone lessons, and it turned out that he had got the instrument for me as a combined birthday and Christmas present.' Dennis, an amateur musician, had learned the saxophone from his Uncle Thornton, and began to teach La Monte what little he knew. Meanwhile, the boy played in the grade-school orchestra, and helped his family herd goats in the nearby hills.

Soon the Youngs were on the move again, this time to American Fork, Utah, where Uncle Thornton owned a prosperous celery farm that Dennis was hired to manage. The Youngs were chagrined to find themselves assigned to an old farmhouse without running water. But La Monte was delighted to absorb Thornton's musical skills, honed over years of playing in dance bands in Kansas City and Los Angeles. 'He began coaching me in saxophone, he bought me sheet music, and he gave me all of his old swing-band arrangements. And I really think that it's through him that I began to develop a taste for jazz.'

La Monte spent four years in American Fork, and, typically, it is the droning environmental sounds that he remembers best. 'The natural sounds that interested me were the owls in the forest area around Utah Lake, where I used to ride my horse or burro. One day I heard a harmonic resonating in the woods, without even knowing what it was; perhaps it was coming off the lake.' By the time La Monte was due to go to high school, the Youngs – now with six children – took a family vote, and decided to move back to Los Angeles.

The family was still so poor that La Monte was sent to stay with his grandmother, who lived next to the train tracks. Not surprisingly, La Monte found himself drawn to the trainyard, where he would listen to the long whistles and the short signals. Soon he enrolled at John Marshall High School, and his musical horizons broadened exponentially, practically overnight.

Up to this point, Young had had little exposure to classical music, or even to the newest trends in jazz, like bebop. He remembers that once, in Utah, he had heard some orchestral music on the radio. But like so many maverick American composers – Charles Ives, Harry Partch, Henry Cowell, and Terry Riley – he grew up fundamentally apart from the European classical heritage. So John Marshall High School must have come as a revelation.

Marshall was a hotbed of jazz musicians, and Young became a passionate saxophonist, finding inspiration in the playing of Charlie Parker, who was then at the cutting edge of bebop. At the same time, Young's high-school music teacher, Clyde Sorensen, a one-time pupil of Arnold Schoenberg's, taught him harmony and took him to his first symphonic concert, the Los Angeles Philharmonic playing Bartók's Concerto for Orchestra. But Young remained fundamentally a burgeoning jazz musician.

In a way, he had to be, because the income he brought in from dance-band gigs helped him to survive. He also worked at a machine shop after school, helping to make precision camera parts. With the proceeds from his forty-cents-an-hour wage, he bought his first Selmer alto saxophone. 'The Selmer cost 300 dollars at that time, so at forty cents an hour what does that come to? Almost every day after school I would go to the shop, and I would be running lathes and drill presses. And I used to sing and whistle along with the drones of the machine shop.'

Sometime toward the end of his high-school years, Young, who had immersed himself in the bebop lifestyle, ran away from home.

My parents and grandparents were very upset that I was always playing in these night clubs, and they were also upset that I was playing with black musicians. I was meeting these Communist Jewish kids at John Marshall High School, and I was going out with girls who weren't members of the church. Here I was the first born, the first grandson; I had been a model churchgoer, and I was going down the drain. They even hid my horn in a closet in the bedroom, but I found it, and I literally ran out of the house with it and left home. I went to some cheap drive-in motel, and I got a job working in a seat-belt-buckle factory.

The early days of bebop: saxophonists Lester Young, second from left, and Charlie Parker, second from right, on-stage at Birdland, New York, 1949

Increasingly, Young focused on jazz – specifically the jazz programme at Los Angeles City College, which boasted a famous dance band. Apparently, all the hot-shot jazz players at John Marshall High School dreamed of getting into the college's band, and Young was no exception. When Young arrived at Los Angeles City College,

he found that he had some stiff competition for the available alto-saxophone slot.

*I practised hard, and of all things I ended up competing with
Eric Dolphy for the second alto chair. How I don't know, but I beat out Eric
for the chair. But I was very good; people who heard me at the audition
said I was like an explosion when I played. At the time I was living and
breathing jazz. That's all I cared about; that's what I wanted to do.*

Dolphy would later go on to win world renown as saxophonist
John Coltrane's sideman. And Young himself was evidently no slouch
as a sax player. Recordings of Young's quartet made during his college
years show that he was a blistering improviser, pouring forth leaping
melodies as furiously as any of his bebop contemporaries. More
importantly, he was already beginning to discard the conventional
chord changes of jazz, preferring to improvise over less predictable
harmonies. It is no coincidence that two members of Young's band –
trumpeter Don Cherry and drummer Billy Higgins – went on to help
Ornette Coleman blaze the trail of free jazz.

Had circumstances worked out differently, maybe Young would
have engineered that jazz revolution. But soon after his arrival at Los
Angeles City College, he began to study with Leonard Stein, then
Schoenberg's most important American disciple, later the director of
the Arnold Schoenberg Institute and the guardian of the composer's
archive. Stein sensed in this unruly and unconventional teenager the
makings of a composer. 'It was literally Leonard Stein who singled me
out and said I was a composer. After I wrote the *Five Small Pieces for
String Quartet* (1956) as an assignment in one of his classes, he started
telling people in my presence that I was a composer. Then I really
began to think I was.'

Stein introduced Young to the whole world of twentieth-century
classical music, especially to the atonal, serial compositions of
Schoenberg, Alban Berg and Anton Webern. And Young became
an instant convert to the music of Webern (whose miniatures are the
obvious inspiration for Young's equally tiny *Five Small Pieces for String
Quartet* [1956]). More than any of the other minimalists, Young had a
fruitful relationship with serialism; it wasn't something he felt stifled
by, and his early minimalist works still use serial techniques. For

several years Webern became Young's idol, and in retrospect it is not difficult to understand why.

Webern's mature works discard the late-Romantic angst of Schoenberg's Vienna, and distil Schoenberg's twelve-note technique into a highly rational, rarefied form. In Webern's compositions, sound and silence seem of equal importance, and the hushed dynamics, the transparent textures, and the extremely brief time-frames all lend the music a proto-minimalist aura. But what most fascinated Young was the music's static quality – the way that whenever certain pitches recur during a movement, they always return in a particular octave.

Thanks to Stein and Webern, jazz began to fade from Young's view, and by the time he entered the University of California at Los Angeles (UCLA) in 1957, he had nearly quit playing the saxophone. Meanwhile, the music department at UCLA opened up whole new horizons for him. Renowned for its ethnomusicology programme, UCLA boasted an orchestra that played *gagaku* (traditional Japanese court music), as well as a *gamelan* (an Indonesian ensemble of metal percussion instruments). One summer, Young bought an Ali Akbar Khan recording of Indian ragas, and was fascinated by the effect of improvised music unfolding gradually over long spans of time. 'I listened to it so much in my room that my grandmother was worried about it, and she eventually wrote "Opium Music" on the album cover.'

If non-Western music was opium, so was medieval chant and organum, both of which Young studied at UCLA. Much later, in

The rebel's identification card: La Monte Young at UCLA, 1957, where he found a wide range of musical stimuli

1966, Young put his finger on the connection between medieval Western music and Asian music – and why both influenced him so profoundly. 'I feel that in most music peculiar to the Western hemisphere since the thirteenth century, climax and directionality have been among the most important guiding factors, whereas music before that time, from the chants through organum and Machaut, used stasis as a point of structure a little bit more the way certain Eastern musical systems have.'

Stasis: that single word summed up all of Young's musical interests. By the time he graduated from UCLA in June 1958, he was obsessed with Webern, with medieval music, and with non-Western music. And he had never forgotten the droning sounds of his childhood – the wind, the transformers, the lathes, the trainyards. All of these musics shared a predilection for immobility, for disrupting our comprehension of the passage of time.

But none disrupted it as radically as Young was about to do. During the summer of 1958 he composed his first mature composition, the *Trio for Strings* – a landmark in the history of twentieth-century music and the virtual fountainhead of American musical minimalism. By the time he began his graduate studies at the University of California at Berkeley in the autumn of 1958, the *Trio* (which had been written while sitting at the huge pipe organ at UCLA's Royce Hall) was finished and was being copied onto translucent paper for reproduction.

Why does the *Trio*, even today, seem like such an unprecedented departure? Simply because never before in the history of Western music had an entire composition been comprised entirely of long, sustained tones. Although the *Trio* is a strictly serial work, it discards melody and rhythmic pulse, focusing instead on hushed, immobile chords that completely suspend time's passing. And each of these chords is separated by an equally prolonged silence, which only serves to heighten the impression of absolute stasis. The opening of the *Trio*, for example, consists of only three pitches, one for each string instrument – but it takes more than five minutes for that single chord to accumulate and die away. (The entire *Trio* lasts nearly an hour, but apparently its first draft would have taken several hours to perform.)

It is tempting to search for the sources of such a work, but in truth it has no real ancestors. Webern provided the hushed dynamics and the

The cover of the published score for John Cage's *4'33"*, perhaps the ultimate minimalist work

dissonant harmonic language, as well as the equality of sound and silence. (Young had not yet heard of Cage's *4'33"*, an entirely silent piece.) The held tones of *gagaku*, raga, and train whistles may have provided further inspiration. But ultimately the *Trio* sprang from the mind of an irreverent, iconoclastic, almost-graduate student. Even Young cannot explain it. 'It's hard to say how I first started writing long sustained tones, other than I felt really moved to do so,' he said recently.

But his composition teacher at Berkeley, Seymour Shifrin, did not feel similarly moved. Shifrin, although an admirer of Schoenberg, was hardly a dogmatic pedant. Yet his open-mindedness went only so far. Young submitted the *Trio* as his first assignment in Shifrin's class, and was told that if he kept writing such music, he would not get a grade. 'He thought a piece should be going somewhere, and he literally said to me "You're writing like an eighty-year-old man, and you should be writing a piece that's got lines, that's got climaxes, that's going places."'

The *Trio*, however, was clearly going nowhere. Shifrin, although convinced of Young's talent, felt that his student could not possibly have intended the notes he had put on paper. In order to demonstrate Young's mistaken judgement, Shifrin arranged a student performance of the *Trio* in his home. By actually giving the monstrosity a hearing, he hoped to turn Young away from his erroneous path.

Present at that première were the other members of Shifrin's composition class, including David Del Tredici and Pauline Oliveros. Young remembers that they reacted with 'polite bewilderment', but the composer himself was undeterred. The performance soon acquired legendary status around Berkeley, and Young says that 'almost everyone thought that I had gone off the deep end.'

Almost everyone, that is, except a young graduate student in composition named Terry Riley. Within weeks, Riley would become Young's supporter, confidant, part-time side-kick, and full-time musical colleague. From here on, their lives were inextricably linked. And the minimalist club would soon gain a second member.

Riley, like Young a child of the rural American West, was raised in the foothills of Northern California's Sierra Nevada mountains. Colfax, California, where he was born on 24 June 1935, was a railroad town with a big switching yard where cross-country trains would change tracks. Riley's father was a foreman for the section of track

Terry Riley and Lynn Palmer
perform Riley's music for
The Gift, Paris, 1963.

between Colfax and Applegate, and so the family lived right next to
the railroad.

Since neither of Riley's parents was musically inclined, music did
not play a substantial role in the boy's early childhood. His Italian
grandmother sang opera arias at home, and he remembers listening
to the radio and singing along with such pop standards as 'Pennies
From Heaven'. But he must have shown some musical talent, because
when he was six his parents gave him a violin. 'I think the reason I
started out on the violin was that it had the only teacher available at
the time,' he said recently. 'By then we had moved further north to
Redding, California, where my father had gotten a job for the railroad. At that time I was starting to manifest a great interest in music,
and I went over to the neighbour's house and played the piano by ear.
So they found a violin teacher and brought home a violin for me.'

Soon the war broke out, Riley's father joined the Marines, and the
family was on the move again. By this time Riley had switched to the
piano, which was to remain his primary instrument. But Riley, like
Young, grew up listening almost entirely to popular music and jazz.
'Because I lived in these provincial places, I was hearing mainly the
popular music that was on the radio at the time. I was pretty much
deprived of hearing classical music in those days.'

One day in 1945 Riley saw a *Life* Magazine article about Charlie Parker and Dizzy Gillespie, and he was fascinated by the new bebop revolution. But he didn't actually hear the music until he got to high school. 'In 1945 it was hard to get records, especially up in Redding; you'd go to a record store and ask for this or that and all they had was cowboy music.'

Thanks to his high-school music teacher, Riley got to know not only the latest developments in bebop, but twentieth-century classical music, including Debussy, Bartók, and Stravinsky. He played piano in the high-school orchestra, mellophone (a valved brass instrument) in the high-school band, and earned extra money by performing in a small dance-band that entertained at parties. But his musical education was still rather sketchy until his last year of high school, when he began studying piano with Duane Hampton. Hampton, a Redding native, had graduated from the Curtis Institute in Philadelphia but returned to his home town, and for three years Riley thrived under his tutelage.

Trumpeter Dizzy Gillespie was a pioneer of bebop, the jazz revolution of the 1940s that influenced Young, Riley and Reich.

Indeed, he blossomed so rapidly that suddenly he was determined to make a career as a concert pianist. 'I started practising five or six hours a day, and I devoured all the classical literature. Those two years in junior college [in Redding] are when I decided I wanted to have a career as a musician. But at that time I thought I would be a pianist, especially after I discovered all the wonderful music out there to play – Bach, Debussy, Bartók, Poulenc, and Milhaud.'

Not until he transferred to San Francisco State University in 1955 did he shift toward composition.

When I got to San Francisco State I discovered there were other pianists who were much better than me! And that I better reconsider my career options. The composition class was quite wonderful; there were a lot of composers, my peers, who had much more experience and were really stimulating to me, because they had grown up in the Bay Area and had a lot of advantages I didn't have. I started composing a lot then because I felt that I really enjoyed writing and playing my own music.

At San Francisco State, Riley studied composition with Robert Erickson, who introduced him to the rigorous serialism of Schoenberg and Webern. Riley's own music, however, was still tonal – what he describes, not very charitably, as 'an imitation Poulenc/Milhaud style'. Meanwhile, Riley pursued his interest in jazz, simultaneously investigating the pre-jazz syncopations of ragtime and the post-bop innovations of Thelonious Monk.

After graduating from San Francisco State in 1957, Riley (who had married and had a family to support) worked for United Airlines, selling tickets and checking bags. Later he landed a job playing ragtime piano at the Gold Street Saloon on San Francisco's Barbary Coast. Under the tutelage of ragtime great Wally Rose, he got on-the-job training in all sorts of ragtime, honky-tonk, and stride piano styles. He remembers the Saloon as specializing in 'fake Gay 90s, with cocktail waitresses who had no clothes on. Its main feature was that it was New Year's Eve every night, and they'd pass out whistles and popcorn. It was a hard job, but because of Wally I really loved it.'

In the autumn of 1958 Riley began to attend classes at the University of California at Berkeley – and almost immediately he met

La Monte Young. Young, not surprisingly, showed Riley the score of the *Trio for Strings* and later played him a tape of the piece. Riley was bowled over.

The main feature of La Monte's music in those days was the total disruption of time as I knew it. It was like being in a time capsule and floating out in space somewhere and waiting for the next event to happen. And I enjoyed that kind of waiting. It was probably my first introduction to a Zen-like approach to the present: not waiting for the next thing to come along, but simply enjoying what's happening right then.

Riley was equally mesmerized by Young's personality, and nearly four decades later his memories are still vivid.

I was really impressed with La Monte in every way – his lifestyle, the kind of music he was writing, everything he did was different. He was extremely eccentric. He was very avant-garde in his dress: he didn't wear any socks, he had this little goatee and a beret, and he had long hair – and this was in the late fifties, way before the Beatles. I had other friends in San Francisco who were involved in the beatnik movement, and I was very attracted to the beats. So when I saw La Monte I thought, 'Oh yeah, this is a brother.' And he had very highly evolved thoughts about music, and I thought it was better than what I was getting from the teachers I came to study with.

In 1987 Riley summed up the impact of Young and his music: 'It's like an initiation. You're never quite the same afterwards.' To be fair, it would seem that neither Riley nor Young were ever quite the same after their encounter. Young, whose ideas and compositions stood so apart from everything he was being taught, desperately needed the unflagging encouragement that Riley provided. And Riley found in Young a musical and personal role model, someone who would create undreamed-of compositional possibilities.

In the summer of 1959 Young travelled to Darmstadt, Germany, where Karlheinz Stockhausen, then the *enfant terrible* of the European avant garde, led an international new-music seminar. Stockhausen had recently been converted to the philosophy of John Cage, which Young had heard little about. 'In Darmstadt, Stockhausen was literally

talking about Cage all the time; Cage this and Cage that,' Young
recalled. Although no music by Cage was played live that summer,
Young had the honour of meeting the pianist David Tudor – the
single most important exponent of Cage's music, and the man who
had given the 1952 première of *4'33"*.

Once back at Berkeley that autumn, Young was determined to
apply Cage's philosophy to his own music. He remembers that the
most influential element of Cage's thought was 'his belief that any kind
of sounds could be utilized in a musical composition.' Riley recalls that
one day Young came up to him and said with glee: 'If they thought I
was wild before, wait 'til they see what I'm going to do now!'

What Young did was to turn Berkeley's music department upside
down – and it was inevitable that Riley would collaborate in this venture. 'My *Trio* was successfully kept out of musical life at the college,
but after I got back from Darmstadt I was a teaching assistant, and I
found out that I could do noon concerts,' said Young. It was through

the vehicle of these midday events that Young, with Riley's help, let loose his latest provocations on the unsuspecting student body.

In *Vision* (1959), Young turned out the lights in the auditorium, and created panic among audience members as he bombarded them with unconventional sounds. In *Poem for Tables, Chairs, Benches, Etc.* (1960), Young scraped furniture across the floor. During one particularly memorable performance, Riley and Young played catch outside while someone mowed the lawn; meanwhile, inside the hall the performers fried eggs, slept in a sleeping bag, played marbles, and handed out provocative literature.

During the 1959–60 season, Riley and Young worked together as composers-in-residence for the Anne Halprin Dance Company, creating further Cage-inspired efforts. Riley remembers one Los Angeles performance:

We dragged garbage cans down the stairways around the halls outside the theater. The audience got terrified, thinking there was an earthquake or that something was happening outside. They had expected that music was going to be accompanying the dance, and when they heard us they didn't know quite what was going on, because it made a tremendously ferocious sound inside the hall.

The breaking point seems to have come with *2 Sounds* of April 1960. In one realization, Young dragged a gong across the floor, while Riley rammed a garbage-can against a wall. This time the audience began to curse loudly; some listeners, in an oddly misdirected act of self-defence, began to sing the *Star-Spangled Banner*. It was a happening that Cage himself would have loved.

But the members of Berkeley's music department did not love it. By this time, both Young and Riley were in their second year at Berkeley, and it had become clear that Young was a real threat to the authority of the faculty. Riley, although hardly a favourite of the department, seemed more controllable. So when it came time to dole out money for the coming year, the university gave Riley a residency and Young a travel fellowship – in essence, a one-way ticket out of town. 'I was too good at organizing and selling my ideas, and I was able to convince my fellow students that there was some reason to be doing what I was doing,' said Young. 'The university got rid of me because they were afraid I was going to take over the music department.'

Young used his fellowship to go to New York. 'When I hit New York, I literally became the darling of the avant garde,' he recalled with characteristic modesty. 'I was just a sensation, and life was so fantastic that I never even considered going back to Berkeley.'

Before he left Berkeley, Young had begun a series of pieces, jointly titled *Compositions 1960*. Nearly devoid of musical notation, the *Compositions* consisted of written instructions to the performer – which, if followed, might result in some sound, or might not. The *Compositions* were completed that autumn in New York, and it is worth quoting a few of them:

Composition 1960 #2: '*Build a fire in front of the audience …*'

Composition 1960 #5: '*Turn a butterfly (or any number of butterflies) loose in the performance area. When the composition is over, be sure to allow the butterfly to fly away outside …*'

Composition 1960 #10: '*Draw a straight line and follow it.*'

Piano Piece for David Tudor #1: '*Bring a bale of hay and a bucket of water onto the stage for the piano to eat and drink. The performer may then feed the piano or leave it to eat by itself. If the former, the piece is over after the piano has been fed. If the latter, it is over after the piano eats or decides not to.*'

Only one of the *Compositions 1960* included conventional musical notation, and that was *Composition 1960 #7*, simply a bare open fifth (B–F#) 'to be held for a long time.' In retrospect, it is clear that all the *Compositions 1960* were examples of what would later be called 'concept art', a genre that Young helped establish. In such works, it is the concept itself, rather than the sounding result, that is of consequence.

None of these *Compositions* could have been created without Cage's inspiration, but by now Young had diverged significantly from Cage's practice. Young would later refer to these pieces as 'the theatre of the singular event', and that was precisely their difference from Cage. In place of the Cageian multiplicity of events that Young had espoused at Berkeley, he now designed pieces that restricted the performer to one closely-defined activity. It was as if he were

La Monte Young with Yoko Ono in New York, around 1960-1, the period when he directed concerts in her loft

'minimalizing' Cage – by imposing a minimalist reduction of materials on Cage's chaotic happenings. 'I think what was really different about my direction was that I was interested in this very static approach,' he said, 'whereas Cage's performances tended to be a little bit more in the direction of a variety show.'

Young had arrived in New York by October 1960, and he moved into an apartment on Bank Street in Greenwich Village. His primary reason to come to the East coast had been to study electronic music with Richard Maxfield, and so some of his time was devoted to attending Maxfield's classes at The New School. Yoko Ono sat in on a lecture that Young gave in Maxfield's seminar, and she was fascinated by what she heard. Ono, soon to become a major player in Manhattan's conceptual-art world, would end up being profoundly influenced by Young's work. Now she approached Young with a novel idea. Would Young be willing to direct a series of concerts that she hoped to present at her downtown loft?

Never timid about his organizational skills, Young was more than willing. Ono's large, barren loft was on Chambers Street, in a grungy part of lower Manhattan (later known as Tribeca) that was just becoming a neighbourhood favoured by the more radical artists of the day. Young gathered a group of like-minded composers, painters, and writers and created a series of mixed-media events that today would be called performance art. Mimeographed programmes warned that 'THE PURPOSE OF THIS SERIES IS NOT ENTERTAINMENT', but this audience was far more sympathetic than the one at Berkeley had been. 'The concerts really created a stir,' Young recalled. 'As far as I know, these were the very first alternative-space concerts on any kind of scale in New York City. The entire intellegentsia of the New York avant garde

– Marcel Duchamp, John Cage, Jasper Johns, Robert Rauschenberg – literally everybody came.'

Ono played host from December 1960 through to the spring of 1961, and Young included several of his works from 1960 on the programmes. In May 1961 Young performed his *Compositions 1961*, which consisted simply of *Composition 1960 No. 10* – 'Draw a straight line and follow it' – repeated twenty-nine times. This could be realized literally or figuratively: either as a single line drawn on the floor with chalk, or as one droning, sustained sound.

One piece of this period stands apart from the others, as it is the only work to involve relentless repetition. Titled *Arabic Numeral (Any Integer) for Henry Flynt* (1960), it consists of any loud percussive sound, to be repeated any number of times. During one rendition, Young hit a pan with a spoon some 600 times; during another he played a dissonant chord on the piano 1,698 times. Young chose not to explore the idea of rhythmic repetition in his later work, but *Henry Flynt* remained a historically important composition, since subsequent minimalist composers took repetition and made it the structural backbone of their music.

Young, however, was becoming disillusioned with Ono and the whole mixed-media scene. He decided to leave it to others – particularly the group of New York performance artists soon to be known as Fluxus – to pursue the theatrical implications of the conceptual art he had initiated. And increasingly he yearned to return to working with genuinely musical sounds.

I was seriously thinking about whether I was going to continue in the direction of working with words, and gradually I didn't so much anymore. I decided that abstract sound was a much more profound language, and that although words were the language of everyday exigencies and practicalities, much more imaginative concepts could be expressed through sound.

No one, least of all Young, could have predicted what sort of sound he would explore. It soon turned out that Young, having already given birth to minimalist instrumental music and minimalist concept-art, would now take minimalism in a direction more profoundly indebted to the sounds of his childhood than to the trendy lofts of lower Manhattan.

Saddened by the departure of his 'spiritual brother', Riley remained in Berkeley, and graduated with his master's degree in the spring of 1961. But already before then he had begun to diverge from Young's approach to minimalism. While Young had been fascinated first with sustained tones, and then with concept art, Riley increasingly turned toward repetition as a musical structure. And he came upon that technique by working in the studio with tape.

Around 1960 Riley began experimenting with making and manipulating tape loops – endlessly repeated fragments of recorded sound. Tape technology was primitive in those days, involving bulky, awkward, monophonic reel-to-reel recorders. His first tape-loop composition, commissioned by Anne Halprin for her dance piece *The Three-Legged Stool*, was called *M Mix* (1961). (Today Riley readily admits that the M stands for mescaline, which 'had hit the scene in those days. At the time I was very interested in psychedelics.')

The raw material for the loops of *M Mix* consisted of speech, piano playing, and various found sounds – some distorted, some used verbatim. In order to realize the piece at home, Riley had to resort to unconventional methods. 'When I started making loops, I had my studio in an old garage, and it wasn't very big. I had to run the loops out into the yard and around wine bottles, so I could get thirty-foot loops. Then I would use scissors and tape. It was really funky.'

Whatever the limitations of Riley's technology, he had hit upon something important: the use of repetition as the primary organizing principle in music. And he began to realize that he was now following a path different from Young's. As he said recently:

I think I was noticing that things didn't sound the same when you heard them more than once. And the more you heard them, the more different they did sound. Even though something was staying the same, it was changing. I became fascinated with that. I realized it was stasis – it was what La Monte and I had talked about a lot in terms of his long-tone pieces – but it was stasis in a different application. In those days the first psychedelic experiences were starting to happen in America, and that was changing our concept of how time passes, and what you actually hear in the music.

Riley was restless after graduation, so he packed up his belongings, along with his wife Anne and their three-year-old daughter Colleen, and headed to Europe. On the way he stopped in New York to visit Young, and then took a boat to Spain. There he led the life of 'a hippie travelling around'. His base of operations was Paris, where he

The sixties art scene in New York gave birth to the pop art movement. Jasper Johns was a leading exponent and often attended La Monte Young's concerts with the other avant-gardists; *right*, his lithograph *0 through 9* from 1960

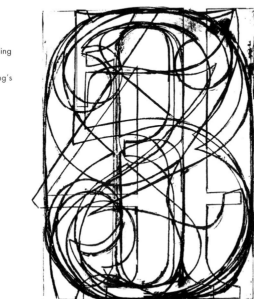

played piano at Fred Payne's Artist's Bar. From there he criss-crossed Europe, performing at the officers' clubs that were located on American military bases. During the 1962–3 season, he even worked for an agency that booked circus-like variety shows; his job involved accompanying the presentations of fire-eaters and acrobats, or simply driving their bus.

In Berkeley, Riley had begun to hear non-Western music, and he had attended a concert by the Indian sitar player Ravi Shankar. But his first substantial exposure to non-Western music occurred during the two side-trips that he made to Morocco in 1962 and 1964. Like John Coltrane, Riley was fascinated by Arabic music's combination of harmonic stasis on the one hand, and florid, virtuoso melody on the other. He particularly admired the sound of the *muezzin*, who calls the faithful to prayer from the top of a mosque's minaret. 'I do remember feeling this is the way music should be played,' he said in 1987. 'It shouldn't be played on the concert stage, read out of the book.'

Riley was too busy travelling to do much composing, but he did have one opportunity to glimpse the state-of-the-art tape technology that he'd been denied at home. Thanks to the playwright Ken Dewey, who had asked Riley to compose music for his theatre piece *The Gift*, Riley gained access to the studios of the French National Radio. He described to the engineer – 'a very straight guy in a white coat' – an echo effect that he sought, and watched in amazement as the man 'fooled around and ended up hooking two tape recorders together. Boy! When I heard that sound it was just what I wanted.' By stretching the tape between the playback head of one tape recorder and the recording head of the second, the engineer had created what Riley would later call a 'time-lag accumulator'. (Simple to hear but hard to describe, it functions as follows: the first machine plays something pre-recorded and the second records what has just been played. Then the first plays back what is newly recorded and the second records once again. At each step in the process, the textures grow progressively denser.)

Riley used this repetitive technique to compose *Music for The Gift* (1963), in which he recorded the trumpeter Chet Baker and his quartet playing Miles Davis's *So What*, and then ran the tape through the time-lag process. But by this point his stay in Europe was nearly at an end. After the assassination of President Kennedy in November

1963, the American bases ceased entertaining their officers, and Riley, shorn of his income, had to return to the USA. In February 1964 the Riley clan landed in New York and rejoined Young, who was now paired with his wife of one year, the painter Marian Zazeela.

In 1963 Young and Zazeela had moved to a loft in a former industrial building in Lower Manhattan, where they still live today. A chaotic combination of living space, rehearsal area, and archives, the loft has served for thirty years as the focal point of Young's musical activities, and it was there that Riley went to hear Young's latest compositions. He must have been as powerfully impressed as he had once been by the *Trio for Strings*. For Young had come a long way since his conceptual pieces of just three years before.

In 1962 Young had picked up the saxophone again, after many years of neglect. Undoubtedly he was inspired by the new modal jazz that John Coltrane had recently pioneered. Coltrane had replaced the standard chord-changes of bebop with long, sustained harmonies, over which he would improvise florid, ecstatic soprano-saxophone solos. Young, attracted to the piercing sound of Coltrane's soprano and also to the even more pungent sonority of the oboe-like Indian *shenai*, chose the smallest member of the saxophone family, the sopranino. Soon he had returned to improvising, but now his blisteringly fast solos were placed over entirely immobile harmonies, reminiscent of both the environmental drones of his childhood and the *Trio for Strings*.

To accompany his saxophone improvisations, Young assembled an ensemble; its sole purpose was to prolong static, endless harmonies while he played. In its early incarnation of 1963, the ensemble consisted of Zazeela singing a vocal drone, Angus MacLise playing handdrums, and a young Welshman named John Cale sustaining drones on a viola. (Cale, then newly arrived in the USA, would play with Young for two years before going on to transfer many of Young's ideas to a proto-punk rock band, The Velvet Underground.) By 1964 the amplified ensemble, which rehearsed with Young nearly every day, was christened The Theatre of Eternal Music.

But by this time Young had given up the saxophone, realizing that it lacked the ability to sustain the precise pitches he sought. He now participated in the Theatre as a singer, adding yet another vocal drone. Performing at numbingly high volume for hours at a time, situated

The Velvet Underground, the
proto-punk rock band that
was influenced by La Monte
Young's work

within the trance-inducing light environments that Zazeela designed,
the Theatre of Eternal Music aimed to do no less than suspend the
passage of time. It would be hard to imagine a musical minimalism
more austere, more motionless, than this one.

Young, however, was not some spacey hippie who sought to titillate
a stoned crowd with quasi-psychedelia. His return to long, sustained
tones had been induced primarily by his new fascination with tuning
theories. Already in his *Composition 1960 #7* (the interval of a fifth 'to
be held for a long time') he had noticed that when the two-note chord
was prolonged as a drone, all sorts of harmonics would hover in the air,
adding a quivering resonance to the apparent stasis. In *The Four
Dreams of China* (1962), he assigned each of the four members of the
Theatre a single pitch to sustain indefinitely, further exploring the
harmonics that would seem to shimmer above the ensemble.

Gradually he realized that he wanted to have more control over
which pitches would be sustained and which harmonics would be
generated. He turned away from the equal-tempered tuning system
that has been the basis of Western classical music since the time of
Bach's *Well-Tempered Clavier*, and toward a system of 'just intonation'
– the tuning that Pythagoras quantified in ancient Greece, and that
so many non-Western musics still use today. In nature, every note
contains not only the basic pitch we hear, but a whole series of harmonics (or overtones) that resonate above it. And in 'just intonation'

the tuning of each pitch in the scale is determined by the placement of those harmonics – so it is not an exaggeration when Young claims that his tuning literally plugs into the natural reverberations of the cosmos.

Once Young decided to pursue 'just intonation', he focused on it with the same relentless single-mindedness that he had brought to serialism and concept art. One day, when the Theatre was rehearsing in his loft, he noticed that the motor on his turtle's aquarium was giving off a low hum, perhaps not that different from the transformers he had listened to in his youth. He decided to use the motor, now greatly amplified, as a fundamental frequency, and assigned the members of the Theatre specific pitches to sustain above it.

So began *The Tortoise, His Dreams and Journeys*, first conceived in 1964 and now, three decades later, still a work in progress, since every realization of it is slightly different. When performed at high volume and over a long span of time, *The Tortoise* rings with harmonics that quiver above its fundamental bass. (As technology improved, Young replaced the aquarium motor with sine-wave generators, later synthesizers, and finally computers.)

During his stop-over in New York in 1964, Riley heard the Theatre of Eternal Music rehearse, and today he remembers its astonishing sound as akin to 'the sun coming up over the Ganges'. He also heard the first incarnation of another project that Young had begun in 1964 – his magnum (and still ongoing) opus, *The Well-Tuned Piano*. Now Young retuned the piano itself to 'just intonation', a process that can take weeks to carry out precisely. At first the piano may sound out-of-tune to Western ears, but over time it reveals a wealth of resonating harmonics that far exceeds those of a conventional instrument.

In 1974 Young was given his first Bösendorfer in order to present the world première of *The Well-Tuned Piano* in Rome; in 1976 he was given a huge Bösendorfer Imperial grand on which to play three concerts for Radio Bremen. (Subsequently both instruments were purchased by the Dia Art Foundation for Young's exclusive use.) Young still plays these pianos today, always insisting on performing within Zazeela's dream-like environment, *The Magenta Lights*. As various hues of magenta and blue are projected on suspended aluminium arcs, the shadows very gradually shift in colour – just as Young's unamplified music, consisting of simple repeated chords or

The Theatre of Eternal Music in a psychedelic 1970 incarnation: La Monte Young and Marian Zazeela perform in the Dream House.

melodies, imperceptibly shifts over time. And time is one thing there is plenty of, for *The Well-Tuned Piano* can take up to six uninterrupted hours for Young to play. (The commercial recording, a rendition of 1981, lasts five.) During the performance, which is semi-improvised, Young produces what he calls 'clouds' of sound – pitches that are played so rapidly as to create the illusion of a cloud of harmonics hovering over the piano.

If this is minimalism, it is minimalism of a particularly mystical, ritualistic variety. Since 1970, Young, Zazeela, and Riley have all been disciples of the Indian vocalist Pandit Pran Nath, and in spirit if not substance *The Well-Tuned Piano* could be compared to a slowly unfolding raga. Young, with his long grey hair, braided beard and loose-fitting robes, even looks rather like a guru. And when he describes the process of performing *The Well-Tuned Piano*, he speaks in radiant, spiritual terms.

Indian vocalist Pandit Pran Nath together with his disciples Terry Riley, La Monte Young and Marian Zazeela, Houston, Texas, 1981

What happens is that in trying to be really tuned in to the highest form of inspiration, I try to not let my mind enter into the creative process. As a result I go outside preconceived limitations, and the music begins to flow through me in a way that is totally beyond anything that I could have predetermined. When I perform The Well-Tuned Piano *I actually pray before each concert that I will be pure enough and strong enough to let this source of inspiration come through me, and that I will be able to make it manifest. Naturally some of the material is stuff I've played before, because that's part of working and developing a technique. But after the best concerts I literally have played things I never imagined before.*

Riley returned to San Francisco in the spring of 1964. Despite the enormous impact of Young's music, he never wavered from his own creative path. Now he was focused more than ever on repetition as a musical structure. And what he was about to do with repetition would change the course of twentieth-century music in a way he could never have imagined.

In November 1964, at the San Francisco Tape Music Center, an all-Riley concert took place. The major work on the programme was a new piece, unassumingly titled *In C*, that Riley had finished the month before. The 150 people who filled the small performance space sat on folding chairs that they placed on three sides of the musicians, and there was a buzz in the air, for word had got out that this was going to be an exceptional event. The lights went down, two projectors filled the room with coloured lights and abstract patterns, and the fourteen musicians plunged into the raucous and thrilling opening of *In C*.

'We were all very excited, because we had had some great rehearsals, and it was sounding so unique and fresh that everybody was quite charged up about it,' Riley recalled. 'And the audience was just as enthusiastic: it was one of those great moments.' A few days later the critic Alfred Frankenstein wrote an ecstatic review in the *San Francisco Chronicle*: 'This primitivistic music goes on and on … At times you feel you have never done anything all your life long but listen to this music and as if that is all there is or ever will be, but it is altogether absorbing, exciting, and moving, too.' Not only was Riley now suddenly on the map as a composer, but a new music, soon to be called minimalism, had garnered its first acclaim.

Riley had achieved something unprecedented with *In C*. It was *In C* that made minimalism a viable commercial force in American music, for it took minimalism out of the lofts and galleries – where Young's far more austere music was destined to remain – and into the rock clubs. It also put minimalism onto the turntables, for when Columbia Records released *In C* in 1968, the LP went on to become the movement's first popular success.

Riley had plugged into the spirit of the early days of psychedelia, a time when communal ritual and perceptual alteration were on everyone's mind, a time when the flourishing San Francisco counter-culture was nearing its peak. The San Francisco rock scene was consumed with allusions to drugs; the Jefferson Airplane's explicit paean to drug-induced hallucination, 'White Rabbit' (1967), is but one example. Even today, Riley would prefer to talk about *In C*'s mind-bending qualities than its technical breakthroughs. 'I saw it as a kind of musical alchemy or magic,' he said. 'I was seeking a spiritual direction for music, in that you lose the sense of self and give yourself up to this labyrinth of sound.'

But it was the labyrinth's unique structure that would prove particularly influential. The simple, one-page score of *In C* consists of fifty-three separate musical modules, no more than brief scraps of melody. Each of those modules may be repeated as often as each player wishes. When a player has tired of a particular module, he moves on to the next, and repeats that one as often as desired. In such a manner all the musicians (and neither the number of performers nor the instrumentation is specified) will move gradually, at their own pace, from module 1 to 53. Eventually, all the players will reach module 53, and the piece will draw to a close.

If you think of each of those brief modules as a miniature repeat-ing tape-loop, you will appreciate that Riley succeeded in transferring an idea from the studio to live performers. And *In C* bears more than a passing resemblance to Riley's 'time-lag accumulator' as well, for the musical textures grow progressively denser as one repeating module gets layered over another.

The almost chaotic exuberance of *In C* is caused, however, by the freewheeling nature of the live performance. There is no way to predict, after all, when a player will move on to the next module, and so the way the repeating phrases overlap will be different in every

A pensive Terry Riley plays his *Keyboard Studies*, New York, 1963.

performance. (Indeed, the length of the performance itself can vary from less than an hour to several hours.) The performers have to listen to and respond to each other, in a quasi-improvisatory manner not that different from Riley's beloved jazz. By so doing they participate in the creation of a work that seems like nothing less than a joyous, devotional ritual.

It was not just *In C*'s use of constant repetition that would prove important. More than any previous piece of minimalism, it also forcefully reasserted tonality as a viable force in new music. Its title should be taken literally: *In C* is defiantly and unashamedly in the key of C, and this at a time when atonal serialism still ruled the new-music world. And its kinetic repetition was grounded in a steady, unrelenting beat called 'The Pulse', provided by one performer who does nothing but drum out Cs at the top of the keyboard. By re-embracing the primal forces of unambiguous tonality, pounding pulse and motoric repetition, Riley threw down a gauntlet before the hermetic, over-intellectualized new-music mainstream. It is no wonder that *In C* became the ticket to minimalism's invasion of the mass market.

Riley, flushed with the new prestige that *In C* had given him, moved to New York in the autumn of 1965, hoping to gain a larger audience for his work. And there was Young, still droning on with his Theatre of Eternal Music. This time Riley joined the Theatre, replacing John Cale, who was becoming increasingly occupied with Lou Reed and the nascent Velvet Underground. Riley, who provided an additional vocal drone, remembers being assigned specific pitches to sustain above the electronically-generated bass. He admired Young and his music, but grew frustrated by the appropriately eternal rehearsal process.

> *La Monte would say 'Let's rehearse tomorrow at 1 o'clock,' so I'd come over at 1 in the afternoon, and very seldom would we rehearse before maybe 6 or 7 in the evening. If at all. ... That was one of my problems in working with La Monte: his time-frame is totally different from anybody else's, and you have to be willing to give up vast amounts of your own time if you're hanging out with him – because he's like a huge gravity center that pulls time into him, and nobody can escape it.*

Terry Riley making live tape-music, using 1968's version of state-of-the-art portable tape recorders

In the summer of 1966 Riley escaped the Theatre of Eternal Music and began to pursue his own projects. That same year, inspired both

The audience at The Electric Circus, one of the top psychedelic rock clubs, New York, 1967

by John Coltrane and Young, he bought a soprano saxophone and taught himself just enough technique to conceive a new piece, *Poppy Nogood and the Phantom Band* (1967). Like *In C, Poppy Nogood* consists of brief melodic modules that are repeated and layered. But *Poppy Nogood* was designed to be a solo work that Riley could re-create in live performance. Sitting cross-legged on the floor in front of two stereo tape recorders, Riley would play his saxophone into a microphone, and the time-lag process would allow him to build up remarkably dense, kaleidoscopic textures. Beneath the intertwining, semi-improvised saxophone lines was the drone of an electric organ. Riley, in essence, was a one-man band – and the 'phantoms' were the echoes and responses created by the interaction of live performance and tape manipulation.

Soon Riley wanted to apply these techniques to the keyboard, a feat he achieved in *A Rainbow in Curved Air* (1968). With its brightly coloured, endlessly repeated, and insistently pulsating melodic modules – layered to dizzying densities, thanks to newly available eight-track technology – *A Rainbow in Curved Air* captured the time-suspending, mind-altering spirit of flower-power as surely as did the Beatles's *White Album* of the same year. (It also provided the impetus for much of the vastly inferior New Age music that arose in the 1970s.) With *Poppy* and *Rainbow*, minimalism had succeeded in eradicating the line between high-culture concert music and pop-culture accessibility.

Nothing made that clearer than Riley's appearance on 14 April 1969 at The Electric Circus. Located on St Mark's Place in the heart of the East Village, The Electric Circus was one of the counter-culture's top psychedelic rock clubs. Riley recalls the event somewhat foggily, as if he had dreamed it.

The Beatles' Sgt. Pepper's *was still hot, because I remember that 'Lucy in the Sky with Diamonds' was playing the night of my concert. Inside they were using strobe lights and mylar and projections to create light-illusions. There was this psychedelic sixties' crowd, a mixture of young people, dope-blowing hippies, and academic types who came to check out new music.*

With the help of an assistant, Riley performed *Poppy* and *Rainbow*. Apparently, his virtuosity on both soprano saxophone and electric keyboards was extraordinary; even Harold Schonberg, the *New York Times*'s chief classical-music critic, grudgingly praised his stamina. Among those in the audience was a young (and still little-known) composer named Philip Glass, who must have been impressed by the cumulative impact of high volume, motoric repetition and rock instrumentation.

Riley's commercial popularity peaked in 1969. His new Columbia LP, consisting of *Poppy* and *Rainbow*, had just been released, graced with sleeve notes that reek of the anti-war, pro-green 1960s: 'And then all wars ended. Arms of every kind were outlawed and the masses gladly contributed them to giant foundries in which they were melted down and the metal poured back into the earth. The Pentagon was turned on its side and painted purple, yellow & green.'

Thanks to recordings like this one, minimalism – a music that had barely been named – reached the masses. But Riley himself, never a careerist, moved back to California and increasingly disappeared from public view. Beginning in 1970, Riley stopped composing for the better part of a decade. Instead, he joined Young in an intensive study of Indian music and devoted his remaining time to solo keyboard improvisation. By this point the torch of minimalism had been passed to another composer, a man who had been one of the performers in the 1964 San Francisco première of *In C*. His name was Steve Reich.

2

A young Steve Reich
concentrates deeply during
performance.

*Stockhausen, Berio and Boulez were portraying
in very honest terms what it was like to pick up
the pieces of a bombed-out continent after
World War II. But for some Americans in 1948
or 1958 or 1968 – in the real context of tail-fins,
Chuck Berry and millions of burgers sold – to
pretend that instead we're really going to have
the dark-brown angst of Vienna is a lie, a
musical lie.*

Steve Reich, 1987

Steve Reich, Minimalist

Put aside thoughts of log cabins, railroad towns, and the immense expanses of the American West. Steve Reich was born and raised in and around New York City, and that environment formed his musical sensibility every bit as much as the isolation of the West formed Young's and Riley's. Although Reich, who was born on 3 October 1936, is only a year younger than Young and Riley, he seems very much of a later generation – not only because his early minimalist language is indebted to them, but because his urban upbringing is so much more of our time than their frontier experience.

Reich's comfortable, upper-middle-class childhood also contrasts with their rough-and-tumble, working-class backgrounds. But economic privilege hardly compensated for the absence of a happy family life. Reich's father Leonard, a lawyer, and his mother June, a singer and lyricist, divorced when he was little more than a year old. His fractured childhood was spent shuttling by train between New York, where his father had an apartment in Manhattan, and Los Angeles, where his mother had remarried; his closest companion was his governess Virginia, who accompanied him on his journeys. 'I ended up living with my father, because my mother was very devoted to her career, and my father seemed to be more interested in giving me time and attention than she did at that point in her life,' he said recently.

Reich's parents were both Jews of European heritage; his paternal grandparents had come from Kraków and Budapest, his maternal ones from Vienna and Koblenz. It was his mother's side that was musical. His mother's father had been in the jewellery business, but he had also been a vaudeville pianist, and so Reich's first memories of live music are of his grandfather playing popular songs at the keyboard. His mother wrote lyrics (her only hit was a song titled, ironically enough, 'Love Is a Simple Thing') and sang professionally. In 1956, she even appeared in the annual Broadway show *New Faces*, which Reich described as 'the one hit in a series of flops by that name'.

Although Reich's father was not musical, he insisted that his son be exposed to the classics. 'My father thought it was important that I take piano lessons, purely from a civilized middle-class perspective,' Reich said with a hint of sarcasm. 'I started when I was about seven. It was sort of forced on me, I had very mixed feelings about it, and I quit when I was ten.'

At the age of fourteen, while living in the wealthy suburb of Larchmont, Reich experienced three simultaneous musical epiphanies: he discovered Baroque music, twentieth-century music, and bebop. 'I had one friend who was a piano player, and he and I both got interested in jazz at the same time, and another friend who was listening more to classical music, and he played me *The Rite of Spring* and Bach.' Each of these made a powerful impression. 'I had not heard Baroque music of any sort, so I was hearing an unfamiliar style. I had heard Beethoven's Fifth, the Schubert Unfinished, the *Meistersinger* Overture –

Reich grew up among the sights and sounds of uptown Manhattan in the 1940s.

Miles Davis was one of the young Steve Reich's musical heroes; here he performs in Los Angeles, 1968.

the middle-class favourites. Bach led to investigating not only Baroque music but earlier music. He was a signal to go backwards, historically speaking.' Stravinsky's *Rite of Spring*, however, was a signal to look forwards. It hit him 'like a ton of bricks. I hadn't heard anything at all of the twentieth century. It was as if somebody had opened up a door, saying "You've been living here all your life, but you haven't seen this room." I just couldn't believe that such a thing could exist.'

Perhaps bebop made the most profound impact of all. Although Reich admired Charlie Parker, it was the drummer Kenny Clarke who captured his imagination. Having quit the piano four years earlier, Reich now decided to study drums. His father arranged for lessons with Roland Kohloff, today the principal timpanist of the New York Philharmonic. Reich recalls that they focused on snare-drum technique and stick control, and that after his lessons he would retreat to his basement, where he could practise undisturbed. Soon he and his piano-playing friend formed a bebop-inspired band, which eventually bloomed into a quintet. (Unknown to Reich, Young and Riley, in far-off California, were also playing in jazz bands – and at almost exactly the same time.)

A precocious kid, Reich entered Cornell University in Ithaca, New York in 1953, at the age of sixteen. Now his musical interests temporarily moved to the side-lines. During the weekends he played drums with a band, entertaining at fraternity parties and convocations of the Black Elks. ('We were trying to sound somewhere between George Shearing and Miles Davis,' he recalled.) But his focus was on philosophy, and eventually he wrote his thesis on the later works of Ludwig Wittgenstein, who had visited Cornell just a few years earlier.

A serious study of music might have been shoved aside, if not for the encouragement of Reich's music-history professor, William Austin. Austin's unique approach embraced early music, twentieth-century music, non-Western music, and jazz, in addition to the standard repertory. 'His fall semester began with Gregorian chant, went up to Bach's death, and then jumped immediately to Debussy and Stravinsky and Bartók and Schoenberg and jazz. His idea was that there had been a return in the twentieth-century to fixed tempi, to an interest in counterpoint, and to a less extreme use of dynamics.'

Austin's perspective served to reinforce Reich's teenage intuition. Now Reich began to understand why he had been so drawn to Bach, bebop, and Stravinsky. For the rest of his career, he would retain a predilection for steady pulse, clear tonal centre, and contrapuntal severity. And even today he states: 'Believe it or not, I have no real interest in music from Haydn to Wagner.'

Toward the end of his tenure at Cornell, Reich was increasingly drawn toward composition, but felt it might be too late to switch careers.

The philosopher Ludwig Wittgenstein (1889–1951) was the subject of Reich's undergraduate thesis.

This tension really mounted during junior and senior year, and I went so far as to apply to Harvard as a graduate student in philosophy. I was accepted, and when I had to actually do it, I decided I would go to New York and start studying composition. So it was a last-minute plunge when I had to make up my mind, and Austin gave the encouraging word. It certainly didn't come from my father, who was saying 'You're mad, it's much too late for this kind of thing, and why aren't you studying industrial labor relations?'

Leonard Reich hadn't approved of philosophy, but music seemed even worse. 'I had already sunk to something that was inadmissible, and then I fell off the planet altogether!'

In the summer of 1957 Reich, freshly graduated from Cornell, returned to New York City. By the autumn he had begun studying composition with Hall Overton. Overton, a composer of classical music and a jazz arranger, wrote many of the charts for the bebop pianist Thelonious Monk and his band. But the training Overton gave Reich was a conventional one, based primarily on Hindemith's textbooks and Bartók's *Mikrokosmos*.

Soon Reich enrolled in the Juilliard School, and he quit playing jazz (as Young had done upon arrival at UCLA). Reich and his friend Arthur Murphy would go to hear Horace Silver, Art Blakey, Miles Davis and Charlie Mingus at New York's then-plentiful jazz clubs, but at Juilliard he was all business. And his business was composition.

He began his graduate studies by working with two conservative American composers, William Bergsma and Vincent Persichetti. In those days Juilliard was a backward-looking bastion of tonal Americana, and Reich discovered the hot new serial works of Pierre Boulez, Karlheinz Stockhausen, and Luciano Berio outside of his composition classes. 'I began to realize that there was a very large vehicle coming down my road, there were a lot of people on it, and there was keen interest in what was going on in this vehicle. This vehicle was called Webern, Stockhausen, and Boulez, and of course I got involved in it.'

Back in the 1920s Arnold Schoenberg had developed a new method of composition, twelve-note technique, which allowed him to systematize the creation of atonal music. All the material in the composition was to be based upon a specific ordering of the twelve pitches (the 'row') whose sequence remained fixed for the entire work. No repetition of pitches was allowed, since such reiteration would begin to suggest a tonal center. As if this system of composition were not mathematical enough, after the war such composers as Babbitt, Boulez, Stockhausen and Berio followed the lead of Schoenberg's disciple Anton Webern, and began extending twelve-note technique to parameters other than pitch. In this new 'total serialism', a pre-arranged numerical sequence determined not only the order of the pitches, but even the dynamics and rhythms. It was this kind of extreme rationalization to which Reich and his colleagues were now being exposed.

Reich's last piece for Juilliard was his first serial composition, a work for string orchestra that used the twelve-note row in a peculiar way. 'The only way I could deal with twelve-tone technique was to keep the row constant, never invert it, never modulate. My ear simply told me, "Listen, if you're going to use this technique, this is the way you're going to have to do it."'

Reich, in other words, was using the row as a point of stasis. But his stasis was not as extreme as that of Young's *Trio for Strings*, which Reich remembers hearing once during his Juilliard years. 'I heard a tape of the *Trio*, and I thought he was out of mind – as did Phil Glass.'

Considering how unfriendly Reich and Glass have since become, it takes a force of will to imagine them as fellow graduate students at Juilliard. But they took classes together, and attended the regular meetings of the Composers Forum. Perhaps coloured by years of resentment, Reich's recollection of their meeting is negative. 'When Philip and I met there was an instant chemical disagreement. I had a girlfriend after a while who had been his girlfriend, and I think that helped exacerbate what was not an instinctively good reaction to begin with.' Not until 1967, in New York, would their paths cross again – this time with historic consequences.

But in the meantime Reich left Juilliard without getting a degree. Early in 1961 he had run off to Baltimore and surreptitiously married, and now he yearned for new freedoms.

Icon of the beat generation: Jack Kerouac

My relationship with my father had become nonexistent, and his presence in New York City even in absentia was somewhat uncomfortable. This was also the period when Jack Kerouac was getting well-known, and San Francisco was the mecca for leaving the East Coast and the 'establishment'. I felt that I had been in New York nearly all of my life, and San Francisco seemed incredibly romantic and attractive. So, like so many Americans, we went West.

Upon arriving in San Francisco, Reich explored his options for continuing graduate work. Eventually he chose Mills College in Oakland, and for only one reason: 'I heard Berio was going to be teaching there, and when I heard that, that was it.'

In the early 1960s, the Italian composer Luciano Berio was often described, like Boulez and Stockhausen, as a serialist. But he was the least doctrinaire and, in a typically Italian way, the most lyrical of the three. Reich was intrigued by Berio's early tape pieces, which consisted of electronically-modified speech, and when he arrived at Mills he plunged into Berio's serial world. (He also studied briefly with another visiting professor at Mills, the French composer Darius Milhaud, but found him 'so old and infirm that he was just reminiscing.')

During his two years at Mills, Reich worked with Berio for three semesters. Although the seminars touched on Webern and Berio's own work, the focus was squarely on twelve-note technique. 'It was enormously exciting,' he remembered. 'It was like being at the scene of the crime with one of the major criminals. There was no question but that I had gotten the word on serialism from the horse's mouth, so I had no lingering feeling that I ought to go to Darmstadt.'

Reich is kidding when he speaks of 'criminals', but his joke disguises a kernel of truth. Although he appreciated the systematic approach to composition that serialism offered, he quickly discovered that he disliked atonal music of any kind. And he found serialism particularly irrelevant to the environment that surrounded him – the pre-hippie ferment of San Francisco in the early 1960s. 'Stockhausen, Berio, and Boulez were portraying in very honest terms what it was like to pick up the pieces of a bombed-out continent after World War II,' he told Edward Strickland in 1987. 'But for some Americans in

John Coltrane, pioneer of modal jazz, performing in Amsterdam, 1962; Reich often attended Coltrane's sessions at the Jazz Workshop.

1948 or 1958 or 1968 – in the real context of tail-fins [on cars], Chuck Berry, and millions of burgers sold – to pretend that instead we're really going to have the dark-brown angst of Vienna is a lie, a musical lie.' Elsewhere, he stated just as forcefully: 'The sounds that surrounded America from 1950 through 1980 – jazz and rock-and-roll – cannot be ignored. They can be refined, filtered, rejected, or accepted in part, but they can't be ignored, or you're an ostrich; you're ill-informed.'

Reich was no ostrich. Like Young and Riley before him, he had become infatuated with the modal jazz of John Coltrane, with its rhapsodic improvisations over long, static harmonies. He would go to the Jazz Workshop in San Francisco to see Coltrane perform, and at the same time he started hearing the repeated rhythmic patterns of the new soul music that was emanating from Motown. And he began to feel that the structural complexities that Berio espoused were absurd. 'I was spending the days at Mills College and the nights at the Jazz Workshop. The opposition between people writing enormously com-plicated pieces which nobody could play – pieces I wasn't even sure they could hear in their heads – and a man who simply got onstage and played his instrument, was almost irresistible.'

It was inevitable that Reich would have a confrontation with Berio. After examining Reich's string-orchestra piece from Juilliard, with its unaltered repetitions of a twelve-note row, Berio made a remark that may have been intended sarcastically, but that goaded Reich into action.

> Berio noticed that I was repeating this particular twelve-tone row over and over and letting it evolve into a static thing, and he said to me one day 'If you want to write tonal music, why don't you write tonal music?' That was a very helpful remark for me, because I saw I was doing what I intuitively wanted to do. I remember, when I first went to Juilliard, feeling a distinct pull between the kind of music offered me as a model – atonal, whether twelve-tone or freely atonal – and on the other hand music of, let's say, John Coltrane, music essentially built up of one or two chords. What moved me emotionally was always music built around one tonal center.

But in 1963, when Reich received his master's degree from Mills, academia was no place to be writing tonal music of any kind. So

instead of searching for a job at a university, Reich decided to try to
make a living as a freelancer. At first he taught at a community music
school, but he found it 'onerous' and underpaid. Soon he turned
to driving a cab, which offered greater flexibility in hours and
more money.

During his last semester at Mills, Reich had become involved
with the San Francisco Mime Troupe, which he describes as 'a kind
of guerilla street theater before there was such a thing'. The Mime
Troupe had its headquarters in a deconsecrated church in San
Francisco's Mission district, and they gave performances there as well
as in parks around the city. Reich recalled:

> They would set up a portable stage and they would do commedia-
> style plays. They would have a pantalone, a pierrot, a dottore, but
> the themes were all political and contemporary. It had a wonderful
> free-wheeling feel to it. Occasionally they would do indoor things;
> theatrical events and light shows were beginning to happen. It was just
> what I was looking for. The audience at the Mime Troupe was other
> artists, the kind of people whom I'd always wanted to get to, not the
> people who were attending Composers Forum at four in the afternoon
> at Mills.

At the Mime Troupe, Reich wrote the incidental music for *Ubu
Roi* (1963), a 'proto-Dada anti-play' with sets by William Wiley,
and he scored his work for the very unacademic combination of
strummed violin, clarinet, and kazoo. (The latter was actually a huge
plastic cone that the local power company, Pacific Gas & Electric,
used to warn traffic away from construction sites.) Later, he reworked
songs of Stephen Foster for *Oh Dem Watermelons* (1965), a pseudo-
minstrel show that the Mime Troupe staged to demonstrate insidious
racial stereotypes.

Already in 1962, Reich had begun experimenting with tape, and
like Riley he was especially drawn to repetitive tape-loops. In 1963 he
collaborated with the film-maker Robert Nelson (whom he knew
from the Mime Troupe) on *The Plastic Haircut*; the collage-like
soundtrack used the LP *Great Moments in Sports* as its raw material.
Much more adventurous was *Livelihood* (1964), in which he hid a
microphone in his cab and, unknown to his riders, recorded their

Taxis crowd New York's
Fifth Avenue, 1962.

conversations. The three-minute tape piece that resulted was a fast-cut collage of speech fragments, automotive sounds, and slamming doors.

But retreating into the tape studio would have deprived Reich of live performance, and he continued to feel that a composer should play in his own ensemble. Before graduating from Mills, Reich had formed an improvisation group that consisted of violin, cello, saxophone, piano, and the composer on drums. (Two of its members would go on to have independent careers: the keyboardist Tom Constanten, who later played with the Grateful Dead, and the saxophonist Jon Gibson, today a member of the Philip Glass Ensemble.)

Apparently, the quintet's improvisations were an odd mixture of academic atonality and free jazz, and even Reich sensed that the results were disappointing. 'My feeling was when nothing was written, nothing came out, because we weren't improvising in any tradition whatsoever,' Reich recalled. 'The more controlled the pieces, the better the results.' In November 1963 he attempted to discipline the group with *Pitch Charts*, a graphically-notated composition that specified the pitches to be used but not the rhythms.

In the autumn of 1964 Reich's improvisation group gave a concert at the Mime Troupe, and one important member of the audience, displeased with what he heard, left during the intermission. That was Terry Riley, who does not have fond memories of Reich's band. 'For me, it was too self-indulgent; it didn't have any direction yet. There was a lot of loud percussion, and it wasn't good enough for me to stay around and see what the second half would be like.'

Reich noted the unexpected departure of Riley, who was already a well-known figure in the San Francisco new-music world, and the next day Reich walked over to Riley's studio and confronted him. 'I was living down the street from Steve,' Riley recalled, 'and I had my piano in the garage. He came and knocked on the garage door and said "How come you walked out on my concert last night?" I hadn't even met him yet. After the initial shock was over with, he sat down and we started talking, and I enjoyed meeting him a lot.'

Reich doesn't remember the exact circumstances of his meeting with Riley, and calls the story of their confrontation 'a little apocryphal'. But he never forgot the music that Riley showed him that autumn afternoon. It was the deceptively simple one-page score of *In C*, with its fifty-three repeated modules. Just as Riley had once been bowled over by Young's *Trio for Strings*, so too Reich was now amazed by *In C*. And he immediately offered the services of his group in preparing the première.

Once rehearsals for *In C* got underway, Riley remembers that Reich 'was one of the real staunch supporters and helped out a lot'. One piece of advice that Reich offered proved crucial to *In C*'s success. According to Reich, 'One of the problems in rehearsal was that we couldn't stay together, and, good drummer that I was, I said "Why don't you have someone just drumming some Cs to keep the beat?" So my contribution to that piece was The Pulse, and my girlfriend at the time played it on the piano. I think I received more than I gave, but I gave that.'

Indeed, what he received would provide direction for what until then had been an aimless compositional career. Not only did *In C* demonstrate that clear tonality and steady pulse could be the basis of a genuinely new music, but it showed what could be done compositionally with the idea of loops. Even though all the players begin by repeating the first module at the same time –mimicking the effect of several loops lined up in unison – they gradually slip out of sync with each other as the piece proceeds. Reich was so inspired by the experience of *In C*'s première that he was determined to find his own way to use its repetitive structure. 'I wanted to deal with that as a starting point and see where I was going to go – and *It's Gonna Rain* was my first response.'

In the autumn of 1964 Reich had brought his tape recorder to San Francisco's Union Square, where he recorded a young black preacher named Brother Walter warning of an impending apocalyptic Flood. He knew that Brother Walter's inherently melodious voice offered ideal material for a speech-based tape piece, but he was unsure how to use it. At first he attempted a collage-like work along the lines of *Livelihood*. But *In C* suggested a new approach.

Reich made two identical tape loops of Brother Walter intoning 'It's gonna rain!', and placed them on two different tape recorders. Perhaps because of mechanical imperfections in his inexpensive equipment, he noticed that as the two machines continuously repeated the same phrase, they fell gradually out of sync (or, as he called it, out of 'phase') with each other.

And so unfolds *It's Gonna Rain* (1965), Reich's first mature composition. Two loops of Brother Walter's speech start off in unison, and one very slowly slips out of phase with the other. Eventually, as Reich layers up to eight tape loops of the same fragment of speech, all sorts of unforseen rhythmic combinations arise; finally, the texture is so dense that the speech has been stripped of meaning. 'As I listened to this gradual phase-shifting process, I began to realize that it was an extraordinary form of musical structure,' he said. 'This process struck me as a way of going through a number of relationships between two identities without ever having any transitions. It was a seamless, continuous, uninterrupted musical process.'

It was also a landmark of musical minimalism, for the entire seventeen-minute composition is based on that single, melodious, three-word fragment. From 1965 until the early 1970s, the technique that Reich called 'phasing' – a structure that was at once extremely rigorous and readily audible – would become his primary compositional tool.

There is no doubt that Riley inspired phasing. But in *In C* the use of kinetic repetition and gradual desynchronization had remained cheerfully anarchic. Reich, in characteristically single-minded fashion, systematized Riley's technique and made it the substance of an entire piece. The gradual process of phasing governs every single note of *It's Gonna Rain*, in the relentlessly mechanistic manner that can only be achieved in the tape studio.

Today, Reich readily acknowledges Riley's influence. 'Riley has been very open about his debt to La Monte, and I have been very open

about my debt to Terry, because I felt in the long run I would be able
to sleep better at night.' At the time, however, Riley was resentful, and
the wounds that were opened in January 1965 – when Reich presented
the première of *It's Gonna Rain* at the San Francisco Tape Music
Center, and Riley did not walk out – have never completely healed.
Riley recollects that 'at the time I was grumpy, because I felt I had
been ripped off. I had just gotten into doing this stuff myself, and
I saw the whole thing slipping out from underneath me. And you
know, when you're a young artist you want to get credit for something
you've worked hard to develop. So we had some words about it, and
at the beginning it was a little tough for me.'

In September 1965 Reich returned to New York. (Riley, quite
coincidentally, moved to New York one month later.) 'I was separated
from my first wife in 1963, and it was not a happy time,' said Reich.
'*It's Gonna Rain* was not only an abstract musical piece; it really
described my interior life. Now if your interior life is like *It's Gonna
Rain,* you want to do something about it. So I felt like I had to get
out of San Francisco.'

Once in Manhattan, Reich found a loft downtown, in a desolate
area of unrenovated industrial buildings not far from where Young
lived. But he felt nearly as unhappy as he had in San Francisco.
Divorced from the uptown academics, who preached serialism, and
from the downtown experimentalists, who worshiped Cage, he didn't
seem to belong anywhere. Further collaboration with Riley was unre-
alistic, as their once-cordial relationship remained tense. And Reich
had nothing but disdain for the drones of Young's Theatre of Eternal
Music, which Riley soon joined.

So it is not surprising that Reich mixed with a like-minded community of downtown visual artists, the same group of minimalist
painters and sculptors who also nurtured Young and, later, Glass. In
order to support himself he took a number of short-term jobs. 'I was a
part-time social worker for New York University; I used to ring door-
bells and ask if there were children in the house, and if there were
somebody else followed up. I drove a cab briefly but decided it was
much too dangerous, and I worked in the post office briefly and that
was much too depressing.'

It must have come as a relief when, several months after his return
to New York, he was asked to compose something. A benefit was

being planned to raise money for the retrial of the Harlem Six, a group of black teenagers who had been arrested for (and subsequently convicted of) the murder of a white shop-owner. Perhaps Reich would be willing to whittle down some ten hours of taped interviews with the Six and create a speech-based tape piece to be played at the benefit?

He was more than willing. The basis for the retrial was the fact that the Six had been beaten while in police custody, and one of the youths, Daniel Hamm, was taped describing how he convinced the authorities to transfer him from precinct to hospital. 'I had to, like, open the bruise up and let some of the bruise blood come out to show them,' he said. Reich took the words 'Come out to show them' and, as he had done in *It's Gonna Rain*, used the inherently melodious phrase as the substance of an entire composition.

Come Out (1966), as the thirteen-minute piece was called, subjects Hamm's speech to the rigours of the phasing process. Two identical tape loops begin in unison and then slowly slip out of phase as they repeat the title phrase; later, the number of layered voices increases from two to eight. The overall structure may be similar to *It's Gonna Rain*, but the result is technically more refined and emotionally more grim than even its apocalyptic predecessor. In fact, *Come Out* is an apt reflection of the horrific racial strife that would soon engulf urban America. The writer Edward Strickland rightly observes that while *In C* 'sounds like a score for a Love-In', *Come Out* reminds us that the Watts riots are just around the corner.

Come Out is a masterpiece of minimalist economy: its materials consist of five words and the phasing process that gradually transforms them. But Reich was feeling increasingly frustrated by tape composition. He said later that '1966 was a very depressing year. I began to feel like a mad scientist trapped in a lab: I had discovered the phasing process of *Come Out* and didn't want to turn my back on it, yet I didn't know how to do it live, and I was aching to do some instrumental music.'

Late in 1966 he made a tape-loop of himself playing a brief piano pattern, and then attempted to repeat the same melody on the keyboard while the tape was running. The challenge was to see if a live performer could accomplish what had been so easy electronically – to begin in unison with the loop and then move very slowly ahead of it, all the while repeating the same pattern. 'I found to my surprise that while I lacked the perfection of the machine, I could give a fair approximation of it while enjoying a new and extremely satisfying way of playing,' he said.

The final step was to see if two live pianists could achieve this feat, without resorting to any tape at all. Reich sat down with his old Juilliard friend Arthur Murphy, and at two separate keyboards they realized *Piano Phase* (1967), Reich's first live phase composition. In *Piano Phase*, the two pianists begin in unison, repeating the same pattern of twelve notes. One pianist increases his tempo very gradually until he is one note ahead of the other; the process now pauses, and the new configuration is repeated. Again one pianist gradually quickens his tempo; this time he ends up two notes ahead of the other, and the new combination is repeated. This sequence of gradual acceleration and repetition is performed twelve times until the two pianists have arrived back where they began.

What could be more minimal, and more elegant, than *Piano Phase*? The twelve-note melody consists of only six pitches; all are

The Watts riots in Los Angeles, 1965 – an explosion of American racial strife

equal semiquavers; there are no changes of pitch, rhythm, or dynamics; and the phasing process, which takes about twenty minutes to carry out, always remains audible. Under Reich's stern intellect, the repetitive minimalism of *In C* now achieved a systematization worthy of serialism: it is hard to imagine a piece of instrumental music more rigorous or austere than this one.

In March 1967 Reich gave a concert at the Park Place Gallery, then the leading exhibition space for minimalist art and sculpture. Run by Paula Cooper, it showed artists like Sol LeWitt and Robert Morris, and the appearance there of Reich's ensemble must have cemented a tendency to link the art with the music. It also reinforced Reich's belief that if he was to find a sympathetic ear for his work, it would be among downtown visual artists, not among his fellow composers.

Reich's ensemble – an early incarnation of Steve Reich and Musicians – included Reich and Arthur Murphy on keyboards and Jon Gibson on saxophone. Reich remembers:

> The gallery was a huge place just down the street from New York University; it was maybe 4000 square feet with twenty-foot ceilings. We gave the first concert where it was 'Look Ma, No Tape!' – where Piano Phase was played in a live version. It was a big crowd, four or five hundred people, because the Park Place Gallery was the hangout for the art world. Rauschenberg was there, all the people who were in his coterie, the Judson Dancers were there, a lot of other painters and sculptors – and hardly any composers from above 14th Street.

One composer who did show up was a former Juilliard associate of Reich's named Philip Glass, just back from several years of study in Paris. Reich recalled their encounter: 'He came up after the concert and said, "This is great, why don't we get together?" I said "Wonderful, good to see you." We got together and we played things of his, and I would critique them.'

The arrangement proved so mutually beneficial that Reich and Glass decided to form an ensemble that could be used for performing both of their compositions. Consisting of the members of Reich's group plus Glass and one other player, the band had no official name, but it served well for both composers. Reich and Glass each presented a concert of their music at the Film-Makers Cinematheque in 1968;

Minimalist artist Sol LeWitt 'actualizing pure theory' in 1971

they each played evenings at The New School and the Whitney Museum in 1969; they each offered programmes at the Guggenheim Museum in 1970. (Not until 1971, during a joint European tour, would this marriage of convenience crumble.) None of these locations were traditional venues for music. Locked out of mainstream performing spaces, heaped with invective by conservative composers and critics, the minimalists found solace in galleries and museums.

Short on cash, Reich and Glass began moving furniture, dubbing themselves Chelsea Light Moving. 'Glass had an apartment with Joanne Akalaitis and their children on 23rd Street over near 8th Avenue, in Chelsea,' said Reich. 'He was doing plumbing, and we both decided that moving might be a good thing to do. He had access to some kind of beat-up vehicle, or we would rent one, and for a while he would run an ad in the *Village Voice* Classified for Chelsea Light

Moving. We got all the overstuffed disgusting couches on the fifth floors of Lower East Side walk-ups.'

Meanwhile, Reich's compositional career proceeded apace. In late 1967 he followed up *Piano Phase* with *Violin Phase*, which thickened the texture from two instruments to four, and allowed the fourth violinist to 'point out' some of the unforeseen melodic combinations that arise during the phasing process. (Although it can be performed by four violinists, it is more typically realized by one violinist and a tape consisting of three pre-recorded tracks.) In 1968, he took a brief detour from phasing and created *Pendulum Music*, an uncharacteristically conceptual work that consisted of allowing four microphones to swing above four upturned speakers, so that the feedback would gradually slow down from a rapid pulsation to a long, motionless drone.

In 1969 Reich had one more flirtation with technology. With the help of an engineer from New Jersey Bell, he constructed the 'Phase-Shifting Pulse Gate', a grandly-titled gizmo that could be 'played' in

A photographer attempts a bizarre angle at the Guggenheim Museum on Fifth Avenue, New York, in 1959; Reich and Glass each presented concerts at the museum early in their careers.

A photograph from 1971 of minimalist sculptor Richard Serra, creator of the controversial public sculpture *Tilted Arc; above right*, the Whitney Museum in New York, a centre of minimalist music and art

live performance and used to simulate a phasing process. At the Whitney Museum concert of May 1969, Reich used the Gate to perform his *Pulse Music*, but was dissatisfied with the result, which he found 'stiff and unmusical. I felt very clearly then that I did not wish to have any involvement with electronic music again.'

The Whitney Museum concerts – one of Glass and one of Reich – were an important milestone in the dissemination of minimalist music, for they marked the first time that the composers had appeared uptown. The audience sat on the stone floor, and in the centre there was a raised circular stage where the ensemble performed. Surrounding them were the minimalist works of the Whitney's *Anti-Illusion* show, which included the monumental sculptures of Richard Serra. Featured in the exhibition catalogue was Reich's strident minimalist manifesto, 'Music as a Gradual Process'.

In this essay Reich aggressively asserted the primacy of clarity and audibility of structure. That he achieved by creating compositions in which the 'process' (such as phasing) and the content are identical. There is no place for hidden constructive devices, or for improvisation, in the rigorous world of musical processes. And the process, once initiated by the composer, unfolds in an objective and impersonal manner: 'Though I may have the pleasure of discovering musical processes and composing the musical material to run through them, once the process is set up and loaded, it runs by itself.'

That description certainly encapsulates a work like *Four Organs*, which Reich completed in January 1970. Never before had he created a 'process' as severe as this one, and it is no exaggeration to state that *Four Organs* may be the ultimate minimalist work. *Four Organs* is not a phase piece; instead, its process consists of the gradual augmentation of a single chord. It takes about twenty minutes for the chord to grow in duration from a brief pulsation to a lengthy mass of sound. In the meantime, there are no changes of pitch, timbre, dynamics or harmony. The keyboardists sit at four small electric organs borrowed from the world of rock, and a fifth player, shaking a pair of maracas, provides the unceasing pulse that enables the organists to count time.

Four Organs may sound dull as dishwater, but in a live performance it packs an unexpected visceral thrill. It is exciting to watch the players carry out the fiendishly difficult task of slowly lengthening the chord without missing a beat – and the chord itself, a dominant eleventh that is common in rock, has a exuberant, bass-heavy quality. But audiences groomed on traditional concert music were not so easily amused.

In fact, *Four Organs* caused a near-riot reminiscent of the première of Reich's beloved *Rite of Spring*. Reich still speaks mischievously of the fateful day when he got a call from the conductor Michael Tilson Thomas. 'He contacted me and said, "Do you have something for the Boston Symphony Orchestra to play?" I said, "Of course, my new piece *Four Organs*."' Reich laughs uproariously. 'What else would I have given them?'

It would be hard to imagine a more unsymphonic work than *Four Organs*, which, after all, is not even an orchestral piece. Yet it was with *Four Organs* that Reich made his first appearance in a concert hall. In October 1971 at Boston's Symphony Hall, *Four Organs* was included in a programme of orchestral music by Mozart, Bartok and Liszt. But it wasn't until the Bostonians visited New York's Carnegie Hall in January 1973 that all hell broke loose. Michael Tilson Thomas remembers threats being shouted during the performance, and one elderly lady banged her shoe on the edge of the stage in an attempt to stop the music. Another member of the audience ran down the aisle, screaming 'All right – I'll confess!' The critic Harold Schonberg, always hostile toward minimalism, wrote in his *New York Times* review that the audience behaved 'as though red-hot needles were being inserted under fingernails. After a while there were yells for the music to stop, mixed with applause to hasten the end of the piece. At the end there were lusty boos. There was also a contingent that screamed approval. At least there was some excitement in the hall, which is more than can be said when most avant-garde music is being played.'

But by 1973, *Four Organs* must have seemed to Reich like a quaint period-piece. For in the summer of 1970, he had gone to Africa, and his music would never be the same again.

Reich had been familiar with West African music since 1962. Berio had taken his composition seminar to the Ojai Festival in California, and Reich had joined the rest of the class in making a pilgrimage to what was then a temple of modernism. At Ojai, Reich recalls hearing a lecture by the composer and scholar Gunther Schuller. Schuller, who was then researching his book *Early Jazz*, had investigated jazz's roots in West African drumming. He told Reich that A. M. Jones's book *Studies in African Music* would provide a good basis for further research, and Reich later purchased it and lapped it up.

Not until 1970 did his study turn more serious. He found out that the Ghanaian drummer Alfred Ladzepko was teaching at Columbia University, and went uptown to meet him. Ladzepko advised Reich that if he were really interested in African drumming, he should write to the University of Ghana and ask to be accepted as a student. A few months later, Reich flew to Accra.

He had intended to stay the whole summer, but illness reduced his visit to five weeks. 'While I was in my teacher's village in Ghana I wore sandals like a damn fool and got about fifty mosquito bites on each foot and got malaria.' Still, his memories of the trip are vivid. 'I was overwhelmed by their music, like being in front of a tidal wave.'

I would get up in the morning, have breakfast, and then go to hang out with the members of the Ghana Dance Ensemble. Sometimes I'd have a formal lesson, usually with [the master drummer of the Ewe tribe,] Gideon Alorworye. A formal lesson would mean that we would study the rattle or the gong-gong, and he would play a pattern, and then I would

play it, and he'd say, 'No, it's a little bit different', and play it another
time. I was recording the lessons, and so it was entirely done by rote. Then
he would play one part, usually the bell, which is sort of the timekeeper:
all the other instruments have a particular relationship to the bell, which
rings out over the ensemble. So he would play the bell pattern and tell me
when to come in with a pattern that I had already learned on the drum.
It's one thing to learn the pattern and another to know when to play it.
Sometimes I would hang out at their concerts and record them, and other
times when they were rehearsing or having lunch I would sit in with them.

Reich was fascinated with the dense, extraordinarily complex
rhythmic structure of West African music, which is built up by means
of *polyrhythms*. The word literally means 'many rhythms,' and it indicates that each player is assigned a unique rhythmic pattern that he
repeats constantly. All the patterns are played simultaneously and each
has a different starting-point; they are held together by the glue of the
chiming bell. (Think of each player as a human tape-loop, and you
will not be far off.)

What Reich discovered was that the structure of West African
music was not that different from his own. His music, too, was
polyrhythmic, for the phasing process results in the layering of rhythmic patterns with different downbeats. His music, too, focused on
rhythm rather than on melody or harmony. His music, too, used
unrelenting repetition as a structural device. His music, too, favoured
a percussive severity of timbre. And his music, too, was a ritualistic
activity that subjugated personal expression to communal process.

But when he returned to New York, he wondered how he would
put his new-found knowledge to use. He had no interest in simply
imitating the sound of West African music. 'What I don't want to
do is to go and buy a bunch of exotic-looking drums and set up an
Afrikanische Musik in New York City,' he said at the time. In an essay
published in 1973, he speculated on how a composer brought up in a
Western culture could honestly utilize non-Western principles:

The least interesting form of influence, to my mind, is that of imi-
tating the sound of some non-Western music. This can be done by using
non-Western instruments in one's own music (sitars in the rock band) or
by using one's own instruments to sound like non-Western ones (singing

Ghanaian drummers, whose repetitive, ritualistic music provided the inspiration for Reich's composition *Drumming*

Indian style melodies over electronic drones). [Here Reich was poking fun at Young.] Imitating the sound of non-Western music leads to exotic music; what used to be called Chinoiserie.

Alternately, one can create a music with one's own sound that is constructed in light of one's knowledge of non-Western structures ... This brings about the interesting situation of the non-Western influence being there in thinking, but not in sound ... Instead of imitation, the influence of non-Western musical structures on the thinking of a Western composer is likely to produce something genuinely new.

In Reich's case, it produced a composition not only genuinely new, but one that still stands as minimalism's first masterpiece. *Drumming* took Reich more than a year to write, and when the nearly ninety-minute-long work received its première at the Museum of Modern Art

Opposite, Steve Reich
playing the small tuned
drums that he used in
Drumming

in December 1971, those attending gave it a standing ovation. They
knew they had witnessed an event.

No work of Reich's may seem as overtly influenced by non-
Western music as *Drumming*, and none has quite as much of the
flavour of communal ritual. Steve Reich and Musicians, now expanded to thirteen members, dress severely in white shirts and black
pants; they stand, with drums at centre-stage, and soberly carry out
the musical process. Playing from memory, they are asked to sacrifice
individual spontaneity for the greater goal of group expression.
Although their percussive, repetitive tasks may seem mechanical, it
takes immense reserves of nearly yogic concentration to perform
Drumming – and that kind of discipline can offer its own exhilaration.

Drumming is divided into four large parts played without inter-
ruption. Prior to *Drumming*, all of Reich's mature works had been
written for ensembles of identical instruments, which allowed the
phasing process to emerge more clearly and preserved a minimalist
unity of timbre. Now, for the first time, Reich broadened his instrumental resources: the first part of *Drumming* is scored for four pairs
of tuned bongos; the second for three marimbas; the third for three
glockenspiels and piccolo; and the fourth for all the previous forces.
Even more beguiling is Reich's use of textless vocal parts. In order to
ensure that the voices remain almost imperceptible, Reich blends
them with the instruments whose timbres they most resemble: male
voices with bongos; female voices with marimbas; and whistling
with glockenspiels.

But *Drumming* is still clearly a minimalist work, for it is harmon-
ically and rhythmically static. All of *Drumming* emanates from the
twelve-beat rhythmic pattern that begins the work and is repeated,
unaltered, for the entire composition. Never does *Drumming* stray
from the tonality of F sharp major, which is the implied centre of
gravity of its opening pattern. And Reich's beloved musical process
remains audible, at least in *Drumming*'s first three parts. It consists
of the gradual build-up of the twelve-beat pattern in several instruments – but since each player has his own downbeat, the result is a
polyrhythmic structure. Once the patterns have been constructed,
Reich turns to his familiar process of phasing.

Drumming's monumental scale is new to Reich's work, but its
greatest innovation is its rich timbral blend. Especially in the fourth

and final section (which brings together all the performers), it shows that Reich has begun to move away from a minimalist economy of materials. Never before in his music has there been such a dazzling wealth of instrumental and vocal colour; never before has surface splendour threatened to compromise the audibility of the musical process.

In fact *Drumming* signals that Reich's early, most austere, and most severely reductive period has drawn to a close. And it is a harbinger of the unsuspected musical enrichment that will engulf, and irrevocably alter, minimalism in the years to come.

3

Steve Reich at the mixing
board, supervising the
recording of his own music

*In a sense, I'm not as concerned that one hears
how the music is made as I was in the past ...
There was a didactic quality to the early pieces,
and looking back I'd say that, when you
discover a new idea, it's very important to
present that idea in a very forceful and clear
and pared-down way. But once you've done
that, what do you do? Just sit there cranking out
one perfect phase piece after another? Personally,
as a human being, I feel the need to move on,
not to sell out or to cop out, but just to move on.*

Steve Reich, in a
Michael Nyman interview, 1977

Steve Reich, Maximalist

In the years following *Drumming*, Reich was poised to explore new horizons. Steve Reich and Musicians, now a separate entity from the Philip Glass Ensemble, initiated regular European and American tours in 1971. Contacts in Germany led to the 1974 release of *Drumming* on the prestigious Deutsche Grammophon label. And Reich's study of African music had proved so fruitful that he began to explore other parts of the globe.

Now a whole new realm opened up before him, that of the Balinese *gamelan*. An orchestra that consists primarily of pitched metal-percussion instruments, the gamelan includes metallophones (xylophone-like instruments whose metal bars are hammered with mallets) as well as drums and gongs. The glittering metallic timbres have no parallel in the West, and Reich, always a percussionist at heart, found himself increasingly drawn to them by the early 1970s.

During the 1960s Reich had read Colin McPhee's classic text, *Music in Bali*, and he had listened to recordings of gamelan music. But it was not until the summers of 1973 and 1974 that he engaged in an intensive study of the gamelan's instruments and musical structures. This time, he was not about to risk contracting another tropical disease, so instead of traipsing off to Bali he went only as far as the West Coast – the University of Washington at Seattle in 1973, and the Center for World Music in Berkeley in 1974.

Both summers were predicated on the fact that I would be both a student of Balinese music and a teacher of my own music. As a student I again was learning by rote and taking lessons several times a week. In 1973 I studied Gamelan Semar Pegulingan, which is a large ensemble, and I don't have very many memories of that, although I did play one of the metallophone parts. But in the following summer, I played in Gamelan Gambang, which is a very unusual music that stays with me more. It's kind of like old man's music; it's the late Beethoven quartets of Balinese society. The mallet instruments are played with two Y-shaped wooden mallets, so you play in octaves, and the instrument is laid out so the note and its octave are spaced exactly a Y apart. They are ear-splittingly loud, and there are four of them, and since we practiced in a very small room, I'm sure I suffered from hearing loss as a result.

Even before his formal studies of the gamelan, Reich's music had begun to turn away from the harsh, percussive timbres of *Piano Phase* and *Drumming*, and toward the more sensuous, mellifluous colours of mallet instruments. Indeed, *Music for Mallet Instruments, Voices and Organ*, although completed in May 1973, prior to his trip to Seattle, is as frankly evocative of the Balinese gamelan as *Drumming* had been of West African percussion. Its four marimbas, two glockenspiels, and metallophone are blended with wordless vocals and an electric organ, resulting in a lush, velvety timbre that possesses not a hint of stridency. Constructed by means of several interrelated musical processes, *Music for Mallet Instruments* seems unconcerned that the listener be

Steve Reich in 1982 at the Metropolitan Museum of Art in New York, posing in front of Jackson Pollock's *Parsiphae*

aware of their unfolding: the emphasis is now on beauty of sound as an end in itself.

That shift in emphasis means that Reich has compromised the clarity of the musical process, a primary tenet of his minimalist credo. Even the fact that *Music for Mallet Instruments* juxtaposes four distinct key areas suggests that Reich was yearning to embrace a greater variety in his music. But *Music for Mallet Instruments* hardly prepares us for the shimmering, nearly tropical lushness of Reich's next composition, *Music for 18 Musicians*, which he worked on slowly and continuously from May 1974 to March 1976.

Perhaps Reich's greatest composition, *Music for 18 Musicians* marks a decisive rejection of the minimalist austerity of the 1960s. And Reich himself was well aware of the landmark that *Music for 18 Musicians* represented. In an unusually revealing 1977 interview with the English composer and critic Michael Nyman, Reich reflected on the 'didactic quality' of his early minimalist pieces, and admitted that his attitude had since changed. No longer must a work be based on one rigorous, gradually unfolding process; no longer must the structure be instantly apparent to the listener; no longer is the act of composition an impersonal one. The bare-bones variety of minimalism, it would seem, is now the stuff of history:

> *In a sense, I'm not as concerned that one hears how the music is made as I was in the past. If some people hear exactly what's going on, good for them, and if other people don't, but they still like the piece, then that's OK too. What I was really concerned with in* Music for 18 Musicians *was making beautiful music above everything else … I wasn't as concerned with filling the structure as I was ten years ago. On the other hand, although the overall sound of my music has been getting richer, it has done so without abandoning the idea that it has to have structure …*
>
> *I agree, as the texture gets more filled up, as it gets richer, it becomes less possible and less necessary to follow the process. There was a didactic quality to the early pieces, and looking back I'd say that, when you discover a new idea, it's very important to present that idea in a very forceful and clear and pared-down way … But once you've done that, what do you do? Just sit there cranking out one perfect phase piece after another? Personally, as a human being, I feel the need to move on, not to sell out or cop out, but just to move on.*

Music for 18 Musicians, which lasts just under an hour, bears witness to Reich's extraordinary growth as a composer. In order to perform it, Steve Reich and Musicians expanded to include a violin, a cello, two clarinets, four women's voices, four pianos, three marimbas, two xylophones, a metallophone and maracas; all are amplified and mixed in performance. Reich now had at his disposal a group of instruments far more varied than any he had used in the past, and he combined them with a delight in sheer colouristic display.

Several elements of *Music for 18 Musicians* are familiar from Reich's previous compositions: the use of wordless vocals to blend with the instrumental ensemble; the rippling, woodsy timbres of the mallet instruments; the unceasing rhythmic pulse; and the constant repetition of brief melodic patterns. But what makes *Music for 18 Musicians* so unprecedented is Reich's expansion of his previously static harmonic language. Reich was not kidding when he wrote that 'there is more harmonic movement in the first five minutes of *Music for 18 Musicians* than in any other complete work of mine to date.'

Music for 18 Musicians begins with a cycle of eleven pulsating chords, rising and falling in volume like the ebb and flow of waves on the shore. Once those chords have been introduced, the ensemble returns to the first chord, which is now sustained by chattering pianos and marimbas. Over that pulsating harmony Reich builds a brief, four-minute piece. At its conclusion the second chord returns, and over it Reich constructs another small composition. This same process is repeated over and over, until eleven individual sections have been built above the original eleven chords. At the end, the opening chordal cycle returns as an epilogue.

This large-scale structure is perfectly audible, but the sub-structures – the musical processes that comprise the eleven pieces – are disguised by the dense textures and the luscious, fragrant timbres. Within the separate sections Reich sometimes turns to his familiar phasing technique. But he no longer seems to care that the process be perceived by the listener.

Like *Drumming,* a performance of *Music for 18 Musicians* has the aura of a communal ritual. Steve Reich and Musicians perform from memory and, instead of depending on the time-beating conductor of Western music, they are organized according to non-Western principles. 'Changes from one section to the next, as well as changes within

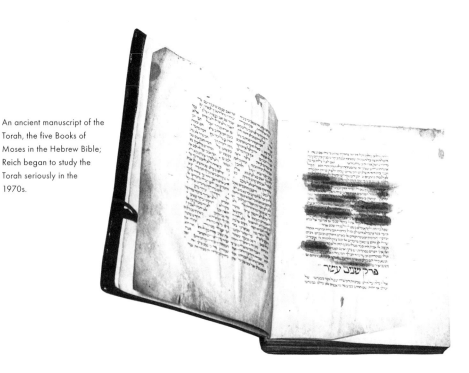

An ancient manuscript of the Torah, the five Books of Moses in the Hebrew Bible; Reich began to study the Torah seriously in the 1970s.

each section, are cued by the metallophone,' Reich wrote, 'much as in a Balinese gamelan a drummer will audibly call for changes of pattern, or as the master drummer will call for changes of pattern in West African music.' Ringing out above the entire ensemble, the chiming sonority of the metallophone provides an audible marker of the music's progress.

After *Music for 18 Musicians* received its world première at New York's Town Hall in April 1976, Reich suddenly found himself being taken seriously even by once-hostile composers and critics. (It is worth noting that Philip Glass's conquest of the mainstream also began in 1976, when his opera *Einstein on the Beach* was given its first performances.) When the ECM recording of *Music for 18 Musicians* was issued in 1978, it went on to sell more than 20,000 copies during its first year of release. And in February 1980 Reich became the first composer in recent memory to sell out Carnegie Hall in a programme devoted entirely to his own music.

Now Reich was reaching a genuinely international public. Commissions poured in, most of them from Europe, which even

today continues to support American minimalist composers in a
fashion that American institutions rarely do. Characteristically, Reich's
reaction to all this hubbub was to pull back and look inward – in this
case toward a tradition that was far less foreign than West African
drumming or Balinese gamelan. In fact, it was a tradition that had
long been buried in his own backyard.

Reich had been raised as a secular, assimilated Jew with little
awareness of his cultural or religious heritage. 'I had not heard Hebrew
chant, I did not know the Hebrew language, I did not know the Torah
was read in an annual cycle, I didn't know anything. When I was Bar
Mitzvahed I did a lip-sync.' After his college years he drew even further
away from Judaism. 'Like so many people of my generation, I got
involved in Eastern stuff. I started doing hatha yoga every day from
about 1966 to 1976, and I also did breathing exercises for ten years. I
became involved with various kinds of Buddhist meditation, both the
northern and the southern schools. And I tried different kinds of yogic
meditation; I even tried transcendental meditation. All of them were of
interest, but I hadn't arrived yet at what I wanted to find.'

In 1974, at the age of thirty-seven, he began to suspect that what
he was looking for might be very close to home. At about the same
time he met Beryl Korot, a video artist. She had been working on
single-channel works, but in *Dachau 1973* she began to explore mul-
tiple-channel video, and she also took on her first explicitly Jewish
subject. Although Reich and Korot did not marry until 1976, their
rediscovery of Judaism became a joint endeavour. 'The first thing I
did was to pick up a book on the Kabbalah – that's where the hippies
start – and I remember having that book with me when I went out
to visit Beryl's parents. Her father took a look at it and said, "How
can you study Kabbalah if you haven't studied Torah?" I thought to
myself, "Now that's a good question."' Soon Reich and Korot began
taking classes at the Lincoln Square Synagogue in New York, which
he describes as a 'modern Orthodox' congregation. They studied
Torah, Talmudic commentary and Biblical Hebrew, and Reich began
to wonder whether he might have a Jewish musical heritage as well.

'When I was studying Hebrew, I noticed that in the printed text
of the Bible there are three markings: the consonants, the vowels, and
another set of squiggles. I asked the Hebrew teacher what these were,
and he said "These are the *ta'amim*; they're not only the accent marks

Opposite, a Torah scroll, the heart of Reich's newly discovered Jewish heritage

but they're also the musical notation."' Once Reich heard that, he leapt into action. He went to the Jewish Theological Seminary and found a cantor who was willing to teach him scriptural cantillation. Soon he was studying from sheet-music that transcribed the *ta'amim* into Western notation.

But Reich, in his characteristically systematic and even compulsive manner, was still not satisfied. His brief exposure to Biblical cantillation had awakened the nascent ethnomusicologist within him, and whetted his appetite to hear the tradition come to life. 'I began to ask the question, "If I want to find the Biblical style sung on the planet today, where would I look?" I was told that the closest I could come was to find Jewish men in their sixties and seventies who were born in Kurdistan, Iraq, and Yemen, and who are now living in Israel. And so that led to my trip to Israel to record these gentlemen.'

Reich and Korot made their first trip to Israel in the summer of 1977. In advance of their visit they had written to the National Archives of Recorded Sound in Jerusalem, and arranged to record the voices of several elderly men. 'We went for dinner one night at the home of a Yemenite Jew about sixty or sixty-five years old, who had a couple of younger sons who'd just come out of the Israeli army. After drinking many cups of tea, he finally consented to be recorded.' Even today, Reich can conjure up the extraordinary sound the old man produced. 'He was fantastic; he was singing through his nose in a totally authentic, 1500-year-old tradition.'

Back in New York, Reich was confronted with the same problem that he had faced after his study of African and Balinese music. How could he, a Western composer, utilize his new-found knowledge without stooping to mere imitation? And again the answer was to be found in studying non-Western music's structure, rather than mimicking its sound.

In Biblical cantillation, Reich discovered a new and inspiring kind of musical structure.

Basically what goes on in Hebrew chant is that each word in the Torah has a mark, and the mark indicates a traditional melodic fragment, and by piecing these fragments together you chant the weekly reading. The technique therefore consists of taking pre-existing melodic patterns and stringing them together to form a longer melody in the service of a holy

text. If you take away the text, you're left with the idea of putting together small motives to make longer melodies – a technique I had not encountered before.

Reich had little time to muse on his discoveries, for he was faced with three of the most important commissions of his career. The Holland Festival had commissioned a large-ensemble piece (which would become, fittingly enough, *Music for a Large Ensemble*); Radio Frankfurt had commissioned a chamber work (*Octet*); and the San Francisco Symphony had commissioned Reich's very first orchestral composition (*Variations for Winds, Strings, and Keyboards*). Clearly, there was no time to lose.

In *Music for a Large Ensemble* (1978), Reich pursued the expansion of instrumental resources that had begun in *Drumming* and continued in *Music for 18 Musicians*. With a total of thirty players, *Music for a Large Ensemble* is so large that it might as well be considered a chamber-orchestra piece. Obviously, the variety of tone-colours is not only a repudiation of minimalism's insistence on a unity of timbre, but also a way of creating textures so dense that the musical processes become difficult to discern.

Octet (1979) is scored for two pianos, string quartet, and two versatile woodwinds who, at various times, are expected to play clarinets, bass clarinets, flutes, and piccolo. Since *Octet* is shorn of Reich's much-loved mallet instruments, the task of maintaining the incessant pulse falls to the two pianists, who are assigned percussive, rhythmically interlocking lines of relentless virtuosity.

In the flute part of *Octet*, Reich displays the fruit of his cantillation studies – a new-found melodic prowess. Essentially, the flute's lengthy, ornate melodies are constructed by the stringing together of brief motives. After years of composing music in which the melodic element was secondary to the rhythmic one, Reich now achieved his very own brand of lyricism. For the third time in his career, a non-Western structural principle engendered some entirely unexpected compositional growth.

That growth continued in *Variations for Winds, Strings, and Keyboards*, a full-orchestra piece whose mellow timbres are due in no small part to the absence of percussion. In 1979 Reich stated that *Variations* sounded so new that a listener 'might not be completely

sure that I was the composer.' In retrospect, it is clear that he
was exaggerating, but at the time *Variations* must have felt like
a breakthrough.

Variations is structured as a gigantic, elongated *chaconne*.
(A chaconne is a Baroque procedure in which a repeated chord
progression or bass-line supports a constantly changing melody.)
In *Variations*, the chord progression unfolds at a glacial pace; it is
repeated only three times in the twenty-two-minute work. Hovering
high above the rest of the orchestra are the flutes and oboes, which
play longspun melodies that become more and more florid as the
piece progresses.

Given *Variations*' new concern with structural harmony and its
increasingly prominent melodic profile, it is understandable that
Reich saw it as a sign of things to come. In 1980 he said that while
Music for 18 Musicians had been 'a summation of what has come
before, *Variations* is very much an open door leading to a much-
enriched harmonic and instrumental world for me in the future.'
He might have added: and goodbye to the austerity of minimalism.

It is unlikely, however, that even Reich could have predicted the
direction he was about to take. Undoubtedly, it was the rediscovery of
his Jewish heritage that led him to search for a sacred text. However,
he had not set a text to music since his student days. In fact he had
deliberately avoided the whole arena of vocal composition, since he
felt that a musical setting of text by its very nature violated the natural rhythms of speech. Still, the Psalms, so full of musical references,
kept enticing him. In the end he selected verses from four Psalms, cast
in their original Biblical Hebrew, and he identified them by their
Hebrew plural noun, *Tehillim*.

Tehillim (1981) is Reich's first conventionally-conceived vocal
composition, but he deliberately chose words from which he felt a
linguistic as well as a historical distance. Like the Latin of Stravinsky's
Symphony of Psalms, the ancient Hebrew of *Tehillim* is no longer a
spoken tongue. And the Jewish tradition of Psalm-singing has been
lost in the West, so Reich was free to approach his verses without the
burden of musical associations.

The Psalms demanded a setting that would remain faithful to their
speech rhythms and yet heighten their meaning. Reich complied,
conjuring up an expansive, sustained melodic language that goes well

beyond *Octet* and in fact has no precedent in minimalist music. (Coincidentally, at exactly the same time that Reich was composing *Tehillim*, Glass was writing the opera *Satyagraha* – his first exploration of fully-fledged vocal melody.) In order to achieve this new lyricism, Reich had to virtually abandon the repetition that had previously formed the backbone of his musical language.

Although scriptual cantillation may have helped inspire Reich's new melodic gift, we would be wrong to seach for overt 'Jewishness' in *Tehillim*.

> *People have listened to* Tehillim *and said, 'It's a Jewish-sounding melody.' And I say horseshit, it's a Steve Reich-sounding melody, and if I'm Jewish then* it *is. But it doesn't have anything to do with Hasidic melodies or Jewish folktunes. The longer melodies are the result of two forces at work: the long cycles of* gamelan gambang, *and my study of cantillation. Together they might have played some role in my wanting to do a more traditional piece.*

Cast in four movements and lasting just over half an hour, *Tehillim* breaks new ground in other ways as well. Its rhythm is no longer rock-steady; although the pulse remains fixed, the metre changes in practically every measure, allowing for a precise declamation of the Hebrew. And its orchestration is rich and varied, embracing not only winds, strings, electric organs, and mallet percussion, but instruments that have Biblical resonances – tambourines without jingles (resembling the small drums described in Psalm 150), maracas (instead of rattles), hand clapping, and miniature antique cymbals.

Yet *Tehillim* also retains satisfying links with Reich's previous compositions. Although it's no longer appropriate in *Tehillim* to speak of 'musical processes', there is no doubt that Reich's former technique of phasing only served to reinforce his veritable obsession with counterpoint. In retrospect it seems obvious that even phasing itself was a strict contrapuntal procedure, since it resulted in the formation of a *canon* – what occurs when a melody is played against an identical but rhythmically displaced copy of itself.

The first movement of *Tehillim*, in fact, is consumed by canons. Conveying the exuberant sentiments of Psalm 19 ('The heavens declare the glory of God'), it eventually blossoms into a four-part canon; each of the four vocal soloists sings the same melody in a different rhythmic position. The second movement (set to Psalm 34) abandons canon and turns to variation procedure, taking a lyrical melody and embroidering it with melismatic ornamentation and new counterpoint. Most unexpected is the third section (set to Psalm 18), which in 1982 Reich described as 'not only the first slow movement I have composed since my student days, but also the most chromatic music I have ever composed.' That chromaticism is turned to the service of word-painting. With a literalness worthy of Handel's *Messiah*, Reich takes the Hebrew word 'ee-kaysh' (perverse) and clothes it in a clashing tritone (C sharp–G) – the once-forbidden 'devil in music'. After the languid, darkly-hued third movement, the sunshine returns for the utter jubilation of the finale. Psalm 150, circling around the word 'Halleluhu' (Praise Him), mentions strings, winds, drums and cymbals, all of which are now brought together for a thrilling song of affirmation. In genuinely symphonic fashion the finale acts as a gigantic recapitulation, drawing upon all the structural techniques of the previous three movements.

Tehillim is an infectious, toe-tapping work that renders irrelevant questions of religious affiliation or musical style, just as Leonard Bernstein's *Chichester Psalms* (1965) once did. It is to Reich's credit that in *Tehillim* he attempted neither ethnomusicological reconstruction nor phony Orientalism, but created a genuinely new work that is instantly recognizable as his own.

Tehillim instilled in Reich a desire to deal more directly with language. A lifelong fascination with the writings of the American poet and physician William Carlos Williams (1883–1963) led Reich to select several of Williams's poems as the basis of *The Desert Music* (1984), a mammoth fifty-minute cantata scored for a twenty-seven-member chorus and an eighty-nine-piece orchestra. Now, for the first time in his career, Reich found himself setting English to music.

Reich searched for poems that he could set with conviction, and in the end he focused on Williams's collections *The Desert Music* and *Journey to Love*. From those he excerpted segments that either allude to music or warn of the threat of nuclear annihilation. Then he shaped the verses into a five-movement, arch-like (ABCBA) structure, with the parallel sections of the arch sharing similar music and text.

A caricature by Ben Shahn of William Carlos Williams, whose poetry Steve Reich set in his monumental orchestral-choral work, *The Desert Music*

Never before had Reich conceived such a grandiose structure, and never before had he been faced with such a large orchestra. In fact, it is *The Desert Music*'s sumptuous and idiomatic orchestration that may mark its single greatest advance. In Reich's earlier orchestral pieces (such as *Variations*), he treated the orchestra as merely an inflated version of his own ensemble. Both the doublings and the roles assigned to the instruments could be less than felicitous; the strings, in particular, were often relegated to a secondary status. 'Unquestionably the part of *Tehillim* and *Variations* which was distinctly non-orchestral was in the strings, which basically played sustained tones throughout,' he admitted. 'So I made a conscious decision that in *The Desert Music* all the sections of the orchestra would get a workout.'

Indeed they do, as Reich transfers the contrapuntal complexities of his chamber music to the full range of orchestral instruments. The choral writing is also fiendishly difficult, especially in the central portion of the third movement, where the peculiarly apt lines from Williams's poem 'The Orchestra' ('It is a principle of music to repeat the theme/Repeat and repeat again, as the pace mounts') prompt the densest canons and most insistent repetition of the entire work.

But the most startling aspect of *The Desert Music* is its heightened emotional range. Unbridled emotion is not something one associates with Reich's music; like Stravinsky, he prefers to distance himself from personal expression by filtering it through a scrim of structural complexities. 'Perhaps similar to Stravinsky I feel a kind of emotional reticence,' he said in 1984. 'I relate to emotion that has a strong reserve, that erects a wall – and then against that wall you feel a force that could crack a dam. I want to control the emotional force, to harness the energy. That's the way to propel the music forward.'

The Desert Music broadens Reich's expressive vocabulary, but it does so while maintaining a connection with his previous works. The pulsing chordal cycle that opens the first movement is a massive, organ-like reincarnation of the beginning of *Music for 18 Musicians*; the dark-hued, ominous chromaticism of the second and fourth movements recalls the harmonic language Reich used in his Juilliard days; the interlocking canons of the third movement result in polyrhythms reminiscent of *Drumming*. And the opening of the fifth movement is stunning: the sustained chords are voiced so as to create an immense six-octave span from double-bass to piccolo. As the bustling counterpoint intertwines within those chords, the visual image that arises is of a solitary human running across a vast desolate plain – a desert at once intimidating and exhilarating.

At the time of *The Desert Music*'s première, Reich warned that the work's expressive qualities did not portend some embrace of fashionable neo-Romantic style. 'I don't have to write symphonies to become more emotional. I don't like nineteenth-century music any more now than I did before there was a "new Romanticism". But saying that, one has a universe left to work in, and I believe that I have more to say, and a greater intensity in saying it, than I did ten years ago.'

Reich spent the better part of two years composing *The Desert Music*, and afterward he believed that he had made his big statement about conventional orchestral and vocal forces. But he never felt entirely content working within the constraints of such traditional music-making, and already in 1984 he began to express doubts about pursuing further orchestral work. He stated that he had no desire 'to become as conventional as possible. Which means I'm not about to compose my Symphony No. 1.'

Indeed, he adopted an almost defensive tone when he spoke of the largely Western symphonic orientation of *The Desert Music*. 'I don't see myself getting more and more involved in writing traditionally oriented pieces,' he said. 'In a sense *The Desert Music* may be the apex of that trend, and now I would like to carry this kind of enrichment back into the types of pieces I've been writing all along. Because my persistent interest is to continue to make a literature which is basically new, and which has as many roots in the radical as it does in the traditional.'

Despite such misgivings, Reich did not immediately turn away from the orchestra. The 1980s, in fact, would prove to be his orchestral decade; in addition to the full-orchestra version of *Tehillim* and *The Desert Music*, he composed *Three Movements* (1986) and *The Four Sections* (1987). *Three Movements*, a commission from the Saint Louis Symphony Orchestra, was once described uncharitably by Reich as 'basically cannibalizing my own, much better *Sextet*.' In truth, it is a concise work that recycles elements of both *The Desert Music* and *Sextet* (1985), but adds little new of its own. Far superior is *The Four Sections*, commissioned by the San Francisco Symphony to honour its seventy-fifth anniversary. Its four movements constitute a Reichian 'concerto for orchestra' – the first, unusually slow and sinuous, showcases the strings; the second features the percussion; the third highlights both winds and brass; and the fourth, of Stravinskyan rhythmic propulsion, reunites the full orchestra.

Still, throughout these works one cannot help but sense Reich's discomfort with the conventions of orchestral writing. His characteristic contrapuntal textures, so lean and hard-edged in chamber scoring, can get muddied in a symphonic setting. And he was frustrated by the severely constrained rehearsal time of the orchestra and the reactionary attitudes of its players.

> *I felt going into orchestra rehearsals like a gladiator going into battle! While some of the players will actually say something to me of a positive nature, I get the feeling that many of them will be glad when it's over so they can go back to the standard repertoire. I'm used to working with a roomful of my own musicians, where everybody is totally into the piece. And because they want to be doing it, they do a better job.*

Indeed, by 1989 he was describing *The Four Sections* as 'a hail and farewell to the orchestra, to a kind of conventional music-making, to the very conservative 1980s.' In 1990, he elaborated further on his rejection of the orchestra.

> *I don't have any anger against the orchestra. I like to go to the Rijksmuseum in Amsterdam and see the Rembrandts, and I think they should be maintained and kept in good order. And I think that Beethoven and Brahms and the rest of the orchestral literature should be maintained by a few crackerjack orchestras well-placed throughout the world, and well-subsidized and well-maintained by the dedicated* alte Musik *community. But I feel that the orchestra is not my vehicle of choice. I wrote for it because it was there, and it was part of the milieu in which I was living, and I therefore fulfilled a challenge. But to continue doing it would have been rather depressing for me, sort of writing music with one hand tied behind my back.*

Ironically, by the early 1990s Philip Glass was writing regularly for the orchestra, and he even embraced traditional forms like the symphony and concerto. And at the same time, Reich boldly turned his back on the mainstream and recaptured some of the radicalism of his youth.

It was not as if Reich had abandoned the pursuit of solo and chamber music during the 1980s. Indeed, some of his finest works of that decade are small-scale ones that carry the torch of minimalism into another generation. *Sextet* (1985), for a lean and deliciously strident ensemble of percussion and keyboards, revives the old minimalist severity of means, focusing on repeated rhythmic patterns and contrapuntal processes rather than on the melodic lyricism and expressive range of the big orchestral works.

The same may be said for the 'counterpoint series' – *Vermont Counterpoint* (1982) for multiple flutes, *New York Counterpoint* (1985) for multiple clarinets, and *Electric Counterpoint* (1987) for multiple guitars. Typically performed by one live performer who is accompanied by up to twelve pre-recorded tracks, these counterpoint pieces live up to their name, for they refer back to a musical process as old as *Piano Phase*. Although they do not employ phasing, they are entirely consumed by the gradual construction of interlocking, constantly repeated canons. And the multiples of identical instruments, along with the dynamic and harmonic stasis, make the contrapuntal processes easy to perceive.

It is this sort of radical austerity that provided the seed-bed for Reich's greatest composition of the 1980s, *Different Trains* (1988). Originally intended as a string quartet for the Kronos Quartet, *Different Trains* began to crystallize as Reich found himself 'unexcited by the prospect of working with totally conventional forces'. So he turned to a newly-available electronic device, the sampling keyboard, and decided to combine it with the quartet. (A sampler, today a standard piece of equipment in popular music, allows a composer to store in digital format a spoken phrase or sound effect or musical selection. These can be instantly accessed by pressing down a key on the sampler – enabling the pre-recorded material to be 'played' in live performance.)

But the subject of *Different Trains* was yet to be established. Reich knew he wanted to return to a concept dating back to *It's Gonna Rain* and *Come Out*, where inherently melodious voices generate the musical material. Now he intended to use the sampler to integrate

The Kronos Quartet, champions of minimalism, pictured here in a performance of Reich's *Different Trains* (1988)

This well-known photograph
of a child surrendering to
the Nazis in the Warsaw
Ghetto is one of the images
that inspired Reich's
Different Trains.

some recorded speech with the live string quartet. But what speech
would he use? After considering voices as varied as Bartók's and
Wittgenstein's, he stumbled upon a subject much closer to home.

> *You know the story about the man who goes all over the world looking
> for the treasure and it turns out to be under his bed? Well, I began to get
> introspective and think about my own childhood. When I was one year
> old my parents separated, and my mother went to California and my
> father stayed in New York. I used to go back and forth on these very
> romantic, very exciting, somewhat sad train trips of four days and four
> nights, with Virginia, the woman who took care of me. And the years that
> I did that were 1939 to 1942. You know the famous photograph of the little
> kid in the Warsaw ghetto with his hands up in the air? He looks just like
> me! I thought to myself, there but for the grace of God – I was in America,
> very sheltered and very fortunate, but had I been across the ocean, I
> would have been on another train. I would have been taken to Poland
> and I would be dead.*

And so arose the title, *Different Trains*. Now Reich had to find
the voices who would bear witness. He visited Virginia and recorded
her memories of their train trips; he located a retired Pullman porter,

Lawrence Davis, who worked the cross-country routes during the 1940s; and he went to tape archives and culled the recollections of Holocaust survivors. These people came from vastly different cultures, but they all shared vivid recollections of trains – and they all had melodious voices that hovered on the brink of song.

'As a composer I was looking for the voices that had really melodic contours. I began editing and I came up with about forty or forty-five phrases, chosen for what they said and for their melodic shape.' Those he stored in the sampling keyboard, along with some American and European train whistles. Then he used the taped samples to generate the musical material for the string quartet, which first doubles and then develops the speech motives. 'All the melodies in the piece were basically taken just the way you take melodic dictation, only I was taking them from people's voices. As they spoke, so I wrote; they gave me the notes, they gave me timbre, they gave me tempo, and they gave me meaning.'

Not only are the frequent changes of tempo determined by the vagaries of human speech, but even the harmonies and modulations reflect the pitch of the recorded samples. 'In broad strokes, the speech lays out areas where the harmony will be. You know what Stravinsky said about the more shackles and chains one has the freer one's movement? Here I was chained to the ground, and it was very exciting!'

All this may sound like mere technological gimmickry, but *Different Trains* conveys a harrowing emotional impact. The first movement, titled 'America – Before the War', is filled with the unceasing clatter of tracks and the thrilling sound of whistles; it conveys 'the innocence, the expansiveness, the whole romance of the train in American folklore'. But the second movement, 'Europe – During the War', is dominated by the wail of sirens and the horror of Nazi cattle cars. At its climax – when a survivor recalls Auschwitz, with its 'flames going up to the sky' – the unrelenting pulse suddenly ceases, and a sustained chord of shocking simplicity fades into the distance. The last movement, 'After the War', attempts to recapture some of the earlier era's lost innocence, but finds it irrevocably tarnished by the intervening tragedy.

For Reich, a newly observant Jew, this is a subject that resonates with fearsome power, and it evoked from him a deeply personal response. 'I think it would have been impossible to present this material in any other way,' he said. 'I did this piece because, as a Jew, had I lived in Europe at that time, I would not be here. It tries to present as faithfully as possible the era in which I survived, and in which they perished.'

Musically, *Different Trains* relies on none of Reich's familiar techniques: instead of interlocking canons and slow-moving chords, there are sinuous melodies, rapid modulations, and frequent tempo changes. Up to four over-dubbed quartets are combined with the speech samples and train whistles, and the unconventional ensemble stoked Reich's creative juices far more than any traditional orchestra had ever done. In 1989, he admitted as much: 'I hope that *The Desert Music* will have a future, but I don't know that I was born to do that kind of work for the rest of my life. Whereas I feel that I was born to do *Different Trains*, and that if I hadn't done it, no one else would have.'

The success of *Different Trains* was due in no small part to the participation of the Kronos Quartet, which gave the work's first performances and recorded it for Nonesuch (the disk ended up winning a Grammy for Best Contemporary Classical Composition). The members of Kronos, with their unconventional appearance and equally unconventional repertory, have long championed the American minimalist composers; in the early 1980s they coaxed Terry Riley out of compositional silence and eventually gave the first performance of his two-hour *Salome Dances for Peace* (1986), and in 1995 they released a disk devoted to Glass's four mature string quartets.

Already in 1988, Reich was confidently predicting that *Different Trains* would 'lead to a new kind of documentary music video theater in the not too distant future'. Reich knew that his music-theatre work would assume the form of a vastly expanded *Different Trains* – that it would now present the documentary material, doubled by live musicians and singers, on video as well as audio. But as of yet he had no idea what its subject would be.

At that point Reich began consulting with Beryl Korot, whose video installations, such as *Dachau 1973* and *Text and Commentary* (1977), were multi-channel works synchronized in imitative, precisely rhythmic configurations. Her method fitted hand-in-glove with Reich's own predilection for layered, contrapuntal music. Husband and wife since 1976 but never before collaborators, Reich and Korot

Steve Reich and his wife
Beryl Korot videotape
material for *The Cave* in
strife-torn Hebron, the
West Bank, in 1989.

had numerous discussions before they realized that their subject would be drawn from one small but explosive slice of the Biblical tradition.

Their music-theatre piece would be titled *The Cave*, referring to the Cave of Machpelah in the West Bank city of Hebron. Supposedly the burial place of the Biblical patriarchs and matriarchs, it is sacred to Jews, Moslems, and Christians, each of whom voice vastly divergent interpretations of its modern-day relevance. Not for Reich the simple-minded artifice of having singers re-enact the Biblical roles. 'To set a piece like this, and have a baritone be Abraham and a tenor be Isaac, would be embarrassingly naïve; it's Cecil B. DeMille, it's *The Ten Commandments*,' said Reich with a contemptuous snort. 'In *The Cave*, the Biblical characters are never presented. They live only indirectly, when the interviewees refer to them.'

So Reich and Korot aimed their cameras and microphones at an array of Israeli Jews (in Act I), Palestinian Muslims (in Act II), and Americans (in Act III), and asked the same simple questions: 'Who for you is Abraham? Who for you is Sarah? Who for you is Isaac? Who for you is Hagar? Who for you is Ishmael?' The passionate responses not only offered insight into the Biblical and Koranic roots of the present-day Middle Eastern conflict, but provided the raw material for a riveting evening of music theatre.

It took the better part of five years to shape that 150 hours of material. Working without a formal libretto, Korot chose some of the most provocative interviewees, and gave Reich an audio tape of their voices. Reich transcribed into musical notation the most melodious speech, and found a logical way of proceeding from one sampled phrase to the next. Then Korot designed the video component, composing a multi-channel rhythmic structure that complements the music but is not dictated by it.

Both view their documentary material with a commitment bordering on reverence and, for Reich, that resulted in a compositional process even more constrained than *Different Trains*.

In The Cave *there were quotes from many different people, which meant that there were many different fragments in different tempos and different keys to put together.* The Cave *was basically a situation where I was tied down in knots, having to make choices of key that I hadn't made before if I wanted to make sense of the English language, or having to give up the narrative and look for some other way to tell the story if the modulation wasn't possible. All of these limits created a very specific working situation, one of the most specific I've ever dealt with.*

Specific, yes, but also demanding. Although Reich's music had been known for its unrelenting pulse and slowly-changing harmonies, *The Cave* was to be based on speech melodies – and human speech varies widely, both in rhythm and pitch. So *The Cave* possesses a fluidity of tempo and degree of chromaticism that surpasses even *Different Trains*. 'I had to grab onto the tail of the whirlwind and be whisked about from six flats to two sharps, and that forced me to make a lot of sudden modulations that I never would have come to – some of which are going to find their way into my harmonic vocabulary in the future.'

Yet it would be wrong to portray Reich as some musical automaton, slavishly notating speech melodies and finding ways to connect them. In fact, he organized the interview segments into a coherent, large-scale harmonic structure that spans the two-and-a-half-hour work. Then he scored *The Cave* for thirteen instruments (four percussion, three keyboards, two woodwinds, and string quartet)

and four singers (two sopranos, tenor, and baritone), whose style is
closer to the non-vibrato manner of early music than to opera.

And he provided himself with large chunks of music that leave
behind the documentary material. In Act I, the original Biblical text,
rhythmically typed by computers onto the video monitors, alter-
nates with the Israeli documentary footage. It is precisely in these
Biblical sections that Reich, now freed from compositional constraints, could create jazzy, percussive music that evokes *Tehillim*. In
Act II, the Islamic tradition forbids a musical setting of the Koran,
so the Palestinian documentary footage must alternate with a *muqri*,
who chants the sacred text. The neat, formalistic divisions of Acts I
and II dissolve in the exuberant, rhythmically-propulsive third act,
where the Biblical sections and documentary material intermingle,
reflecting the freewheeling and irreverent American responses to the
religious tradition.

The Cave received its world première at the Vienna Festival in May
1993, and its American première at the Brooklyn Academy of Music in
October 1993. Controversy flared over how to categorize it, and Reich
himself seemed to delight in making inflammatory pronouncements.
In 1993 he was sure of one thing: he would not describe *The Cave* as an
opera. 'If you want to call *The Cave* an opera in the sense that "opera"
means "work", then of course it's an opera,' he said. 'But if you want
to call it an opera in the sense that there's an orchestra in the pit and
bel canto singers onstage, then it certainly is not an opera.'

Reich and Korot preferred to call *The Cave* 'an entirely new
kind of music theater', a phrase that reeks of publicity hype but is
absolutely accurate. Instead of rehashing the conventions of opera yet
again, Reich and Korot constructed a unique hybrid – not quite music
video, not quite docudrama, not quite opera, but owing something to
them all. With its razor-sharp, computer-driven synchronization of
music and video, *The Cave* is a profoundly original theatrical vision.

To have supported this structure with conventional operatic forces
seemed to Reich the height of absurdity. In fact, he has little respect
for an opera such as John Adams's *Nixon in China*, which takes a contemporary subject but clothes it in traditional garb.

I question the validity of doing operas in the 1990s using the same
bel canto *voice and the same orchestra that Mozart or Verdi would have*

used. If you have a reason to do that, as Stravinsky did in The Rake's Progress, *then fine, because you're trying to conjure up Mozart. But I don't see the same necessity in the operas of my contemporaries, which seem to simply say, 'Well, these are the vocal and orchestral resources they've got in Houston or New York, and that's what I'll use.' That seems to me more like a marriage-of-convenience than real thinking.*

In Reich's view, a subject as contemporary as *The Cave* demanded musical resources that speak in the language of our day – an electrified onstage band, and a foursome of amplified vocalists who sound more like Ella Fitzgerald than Joan Sutherland. Such radicalism certainly has not endeared Reich to the power-brokers of the opera world, who are notoriously skittish when it comes to electronics and amplification.

And there is no doubt that Reich's music itself, so rigorously austere and mistrustful of theatrical histrionics, does not lend itself naturally to the demands of opera. One cannot help but recall an offhand remark that Reich made in 1986, when he stated: 'I am not, like Glass, a theater composer; I don't carry the theater around inside me.' Indeed, there is something profoundly anti-dramatic about *The Cave*. Neither narrative nor non-narrative, it lacks the cumulative, directionalized power of much music-theatre, and can seem static and didactic, a sort of documentary with synchronized music.

Still, it is to Reich's credit that he chose to question the conventions of opera at every stage of the creative process. If *The Cave* is not an unqualified success, it stands as a bold and visionary attempt to create a new, twenty-first-century variety of music theatre. What Reich could not have anticipated was the tragic confrontation of artistic creation and grim, political reality.

On the morning of 25 February 1994, a Jewish religious fanatic from the Israeli settlement of Qiryat Arba took a ride to nearby Hebron. He went straight to the Cave of Machpelah, where he committed one of the worst massacres in recent Middle Eastern history – the murder of twenty-nine Muslim worshippers who were praying at the mosque inside. Prior to the slaughter, *The Cave* had not sparked any political controversy. 'We were terribly concerned about it, but the upshot of it was a total zero,' said Reich. 'And there were many Arabs who saw it, in America as well as Europe.'

Now, with the première of *The Cave* just past, the massacre came
as a horrifying aftershock. Reich and Korot responded to the atrocity
in a *New York Times* article titled 'Thoughts About the Madness in
Abraham's Cave.' There they restated Reich's deeply-held belief that
art, although a reflection of political concerns, can have no impact on
the actual course of world events. They wrote:

> *We do not think that* The Cave *or any other artwork can directly
> effect peace in the Middle East. Pablo Picasso's* Guernica *had no effect on
> the aerial bombing of civilians, nor did the works of Kurt Weill, Bertolt
> Brecht and many other artists stop the rise of Hitler. These works live …
> through the quality of their artistry, and some individuals who see or hear
> them can be changed by the experience, as if a fire in the mind of one
> lighted a fire in the mind of another.*

Reich and Korot live and work in a renovated industrial building
across the street from City Hall, not far from the Lower Manhattan
lofts and galleries where minimalism first caught fire in the mid-1960s.
Reich's small studio is engulfed by tape equipment, computers, an
upright piano, and a particularly prominent xylophone.

This unceasingly energetic, fiercely articulate composer talks
urgently, his words pouring forth in bushel-size paragraphs. Like his
music, he is rarely demonstrative; his passion comes through by means
of intellect, not emotion. Although Reich's dry, even caustic wit can
turn on himself, he is a man of strong opinions – which he delivers
unreservedly and with unflinching honesty.

By devoting five years to a project as immense as *The Cave*, Reich
took a calculated risk. Was he concerned about the commercial ramifi-
cations of his prolonged compositional silence?

> *Sure I worried about it. My thoughts were that* The Cave *better be a
> success. But you have to do what you have to do. I wanted to solve the
> problem of music theater for myself, and I thought I really had it right
> and it turned out to be very long project. It didn't cost me anything in
> Europe, but it may have cost me something in America. And I think it has
> been compounded by the fact that* The Cave *is very difficult and expensive
> to do in America.*

Left, Steve Reich and Beryl Korot, co-creators of *The Cave,* before its American première in 1993; *below,* Steve Reich in the studio of Stuttgart Radio, 1986

In America, which lacks state-subsidized theatres, *The Cave* is prohibitively expensive; it costs $200,000 each time it is mounted. The fact that not a single American opera house restaged it after its New York première is certainly a reflection of that fact. But it may reflect another, even harsher reality – that Reich no longer possesses the commercial appeal of Philip Glass. Neither a composer of instantly accessible scores, nor a collaborator with world-renowned figures from popular culture, Reich and his music have become something of a specialized taste.

That, of course, is not a reflection of the value of his work, and in fact it speaks well for the originality of his achievement. Indeed, it is Reich and Young who have turned out to be the most uncompromising of the first-generation minimalists, preferring to follow their own, often thorny, inner visions than the fashionable trends of the day. 'Some of my contemporaries are content to write old-fashioned works, and there's a real place for that,' Reich said with a sigh. 'I'm just not that kind of composer. My best work questions convention.'

For Reich, composing is a slow, painstaking and methodical process. Temperamentally unsuited for taking on a large number of commissions, he allows himself plenty of time to realize the few projects that interest him. Since until recently he has avoided the high-profile world of music-theatre, he has effectively ceded the limelight to those who have worked more continuously in that arena.

And no one has devoted more time and energy to opera and music-theatre than a composer named Philip Glass.

4

A young and moody Philip
Glass, pictured here in Paris,
1965

*At the point where I was really working with
repetitive structures and simple pitch relationships and approached other musicians with it,
they actually became quite angry and wouldn't
play it. Originally, I was unprepared for that
[anger]. It seemed to me that the music was so
simple, so transparent, what was there to be
angry about? Of course, that was precisely what
there was to be angry about. I had, perhaps
without intending it ..., challenged so many
precepts of the modernist tradition.*

Philip Glass, 1980

Philip Glass, Minimalist

SWATCH TEST № 34.

..........PUNCTUALITY..........

MUSICALL

ITS MELODIES COMPOSED BY PHILIP
GLASS MAKE ROMANTIC
APPOINTMENTS MORE PLEASURABLE
AND THOSE AT THE DENTIST
A LITTLE LESS DRAMATIC.
IN BOTH CASES IT HELPS YOU TO GET
THERE ON TIME. MUSICALL:
THE RIGHT SOUND AT THE RIGHT TIME.

Composer as commodity: an
advertisement for the Philip
Glass Swatch watch

Philip Glass is more than just a composer. By the 1990s, he has attained the enviable status of mass-culture phenomenon. No living composer has sold more recordings and become such a force in a larger cultural arena outside the classical-music ghetto. In an age when composers tend to operate on the marginalized fringe of society, Glass is a happy exception, possessing a huge and trendy audience that blends fans of rock-and-roll, New Age, and classical music. Indeed, he has become a cultural icon in his own right. Philip Glass drinks *Cutty Sark* Scotch, proclaimed one advertisement. Philip Glass wrote a melody to be played by a Swatch watch's electronic chip, announced a press release. When has a living composer ever been a sought-after marketing commodity?

Glass's status is so unique that it is worth remembering that he had an entirely conventional musical upbringing. Born on 31 January 1937 in Baltimore, the grandson of Jewish immigrants from Lithuania and Russia, Glass received his earliest musical exposure from his father Ben, who ran a radio repair shop. But Ben Glass did not just service radios; he also sold recordings. When certain discs languished in the bins, unsold, he would bring them home and play them for his three children. In such a manner, Glass heard Schubert's Piano Trio in E flat major (his earliest musical memory, from the age of four), Beethoven string quartets, and later the Elliott Carter quartets and Shostakovich symphonies. By the age of twelve, Glass was working in his father's record department, where he got to listen to a wide range of music, both classical and popular.

He had already demonstrated a precocious musical talent. At the age of six he began studying the violin; soon he switched to the flute and was accepted as a student in the Peabody Conservatory's preparatory division. But he became frustrated with the limited repertory of the flute and switched again, this time to the piano. At the tender age of fourteen he passed an early entrance exam for the University of Chicago, and he began his studies there in the autumn of 1952, when he was only fifteen.

In Chicago he majored not in music but in mathematics and philosophy; in his spare time he wrestled, practised the piano, and introduced himself to the music of Ives and Webern. In order to support himself, he took part-time jobs waiting on tables and loading cargo onto airplanes. By the time he graduated in June 1956 at the age of nineteen, he had begun to compose. Like Young in far-off California, Glass was most impressed by the serialism of Webern – and his study of Webern similarly inspired a twelve-note string trio, composed before he left Chicago.

In 1954 Glass had visited Paris to study French, and he briefly immersed himself in the demi-monde of Jean Cocteau. 'The bohemian life you see in [Cocteau's] *Orphée* was the life that I knew and was attracted to, and those characters were the people I hung out with,' he recalled in 1994. 'I visited painters' studios and saw their work and I went to the Beaux Arts ball and stayed up all night and ran around.' Little did he suspect that he would return to Paris exactly a decade later, or that his 1964 trip would have far more historic consequences.

Like Reich, Glass moved on to the Juilliard School, and he too turned to composition. Not only were Glass and Reich classmates, but they studied with the same teachers, William Bergsma and Vincent Persichetti. Glass did not stir up trouble at Juilliard, as Young was busy doing in Berkeley. Instead, he was a model composition student. Having abandoned his earlier interest in serialism, he now turned to a tonal style redolent of Copland and William Schuman – an idiom that fitted perfectly with Juilliard's predilection for Americana.

'I was a very good student; I was an A+ student, and those were A+ pieces,' he said in 1980. 'I learned composition at that time by imitating my teachers, and they loved it; it was a kind of homage to them ... The best thing for me to say is that those [pieces] were written by somebody else. I don't think it's worth anybody's time to bother with that music.'

Glass certainly was productive during his Juilliard period. Of some seventy works he composed, most were performed and, because of Persichetti's contacts, many were published by Elkan-Vogel. 'Little did I know that those pieces would be, if not embarrassing, certainly non-representative. If I could get those pieces back from the publisher, I would.'

Of course there was more to musical life in New York than just Juilliard. Like Reich, Glass went downtown to the Village Vanguard to hear John Coltrane, although he was far less influenced by jazz than Young, Riley or Reich. Quite by chance, he even attended one of Yoko Ono's loft concerts in May 1961, precisely the evening when Young was performing his *Compositions 1961*. 'He wasn't playing music, he was just drawing a line,' said Glass. 'I thought it was amazing that anybody would do that. That was very avant-garde to me at the age of twenty-three. I was shocked by it and I remembered it.'

During the summer of 1960, Glass had visited Aspen, Colorado, where he studied with Darius Milhaud. A year later, Milhaud would teach Reich at Mills College, and Reich would come away unimpressed. But in 1960 Milhaud still possessed some of his old spark. Already betraying his Francophile orientation, Glass questioned Milhaud about Paris in the 1920s and 1930s, and about his collaborations with Cocteau. He also continued to demonstrate his remarkable compositional facility, writing and orchestrating an entire Violin Concerto under Milhaud's tutelage.

One gets the sense that Glass was leading the respectable, somewhat insular life of a conservatory composition student, and things did not change much after he received his master's degree from Juilliard in 1961. From 1962 to 1964 he lived in Pittsburgh, having been the beneficiary of a Ford Foundation programme that placed young composers in public schools. Now his job was to churn out *Gebrauchsmusik*, pieces that would be useful for amateur school performances. His compositions, mostly in a tonal, Coplandesque idiom, included marches for school band, a *Convention Overture* for community orchestra, a 'moderately difficult' string quartet, and other chamber works. More than twenty of these were published by Elkan-Vogel, and all of them have long since been disowned by the composer.

So at the age of twenty-seven, Glass was a working composer and a productive member of society, able to write easily in a style that would offend no-one. There was absolutely nothing about his career that suggested the radical direction he would pursue only a few years later. By 1964 Young had organized his Theatre of Eternal Music, Riley was working on *In C*, Reich was experimenting with tape loops – and Glass was still composing conventional Americana.

He must have sensed that he had reached a dead end, for in 1964 he decided to begin his compositional training all over again. And what better place to do it than in Paris? Thanks to a two-year Fulbright fellowship, he was able to travel to France to study with Nadia Boulanger – the most renowned composition teacher of the twentieth century, the woman who single-handedly taught generations of American composers, beginning with Aaron Copland and Virgil Thomson. No one was better equipped than Boulanger to give Glass the rigorous technique that he felt he lacked. Boulanger was legendary for her brutal contrapuntal regime, and in the past Glass has described her as a 'monster'. Today he looks back on those days more charitably, admitting that 'I couldn't write the music I'm writing today without the technical mastery of basic com-positional skills that I learned with her.' Still, Glass's recollections of his studies reveal the fearsome level of discipline she demanded. In his 1987 autobiography, *Music by Philip Glass*, he wrote:

For Boulanger, my Juilliard achievements didn't count at all.
I remember the first afternoon I spent with her at her apartment/studio on

Philip Glass and Joanne
Akalaitis, later his first wife,
on the beach in Spain, in
the summer of 1964

Glass's teacher in Paris,
Nadia Boulanger, much
admired and much feared

*the Rue Ballou. She was seventy-nine at the time, a tough, aristocratic
Frenchwoman elegantly dressed in fashions fifty years out of date.
In dead silence, she read through pages and pages of the music I had
brought her. I think I must have been quite proud of some of it.
Finally, after an eternity of silent perusal, she pounced on a measure,
pointing triumphantly at it, and declared: 'There. This was written
by a real composer.'*

*That was the first and last time she said anything nice to me for the
next two years.*

*From that day on, she set me on a program that started with begin-
ner's lessons in counterpoint and harmony and continued with analysis of
music, ear training, score reading, and anything else she could think of.
Her pedagogy was thorough and relentless. From a young man of twenty-
six [sic], I became a child again, relearning everything from the
beginning. But when I left Paris in the fall of 1966, I had remade my
technique and had learned to hear in a way that would have been
unimaginable to me only a few years before.*

Glass saw Boulanger three times a week, once for his private
lesson, once for her general classes (which were open to anyone who
had studied with her), and once for the infamous 'Black Thursday'

session, which was custom-tailored to challenge (and torture) a half dozen specially chosen students. One day in 1965 Glass appeared for his harmony lesson, bringing with him an assignment he had completed:

She saw an error in something called hidden parallel fifths. She studied the page in silence and then turned toward me. With a look of understanding and compassion she asked how I was feeling. I said, 'I'm feeling fine, Mademoiselle.' She asked, 'Do you have a fever? Do you have a headache?' And I didn't know what was going on. 'I know of a good psychiatrist. Seeing a therapist can be very confidential, and one need not be embarrassed at all.' I explained that I didn't need that kind of help. Finally she said 'Well I don't understand' ... Then she wheeled around and pointed at the mistake I had made. 'How else do you explain the state of mind that produced this error? You're so distracted, so out of touch with reality; if you were really conscious of what you were doing, this could not have happened.'

At least the musicians whom Boulanger held up as models were composers whom Glass liked – primarily Palestrina, Monteverdi and Mozart. That was more than he could say for the contemporary music scene in Paris, which was dominated by the fanatical serialism of Pierre Boulez. In 1984 he referred to Boulez's new-music series, the *Domaine Musicale*, as 'a wasteland, dominated by these maniacs, these creeps, who were trying to make everyone write this crazy creepy music.' Glass, after all, had already studied serialism as a teenager in Chicago, and had long since lost interest in atonality of any kind. 'To me, it was music of the past passing itself off as music of the present. After all, Arnold Schoenberg was about the same age as my grandfather!'

During Glass's second year with Boulanger, a fortuitous circumstance suddenly broadened his musical horizons. In the autumn of 1965, he was hired by the film-maker Conrad Rooks to act as music director for the movie *Chappaqua* (which the writer Edward Strickland has eloquently described as an 'acid-head epic'). Not only did Glass have to compose his own score, but he had to transcribe into Western notation the music that the Indian sitarist Ravi Shankar was writing for other sections of the film. Without Glass's transcriptions, the French musicians who were to record the sound-track would be unable to learn Shankar's score. And the task was being assigned to a young composer who, by his own admission, knew virtually nothing about non-Western music.

Glass spent several months with Shankar and his tabla player, Alla Rakha. Gradually he learned that Indian music was structured according to rhythmic principles very different from those of the West. As Glass understood it, Indian rhythmic structures were built up by an additive process, one in which single beats are strung together to create longer rhythmic cycles. In *Music by Philip Glass*, he described his discovery:

Alla Rakha, tabla, and Ravi Shankar, sitar, who introduced Glass to the complexities of Indian music

> *I would explain the difference between the use of rhythm in Western and Indian music in the following way: in Western music we divide time – as if you were to take a length of time and slice it the way you slice a loaf of bread. In Indian music (and all the non-Western music with which I'm familiar), you take small units, or 'beats', and string them together to make up larger time values.*

This was brought home to me quite powerfully while working with Ravi and Alla Rakha in the recording studio. There we were with the musicians sitting around waiting for me to notate the music to be recorded … [Ravi] would sing the music to me, and I would write it down, part by part … The problem came when I placed bar lines in the music as we normally do in Western music. This created unwarranted accents. When the music was played back, Alla Rakha caught the error right away. No matter where I placed the bar line (thereby 'dividing' the music in the regular Western style), he would catch me.

'All the notes are equal,' he kept piping at me …

Finally, in desperation, I dropped the bar lines altogether. And there, before my eyes, I could see what Alla Rakha had been trying to tell me. Instead of distinct groupings of eighth notes, a steady stream of rhythmic pulses stood revealed.

That steady stream of pulses would soon become the backbone of Glass's own music. The first evidence of his newly reductive, rhythmically repetitive idiom surfaced in the incidental music he wrote for a 1965 Paris staging of Samuel Beckett's *Play*. Directed by Lee Breuer, *Play* was one of the first productions to be offered by an American experimental theatre collective that, after its return to New York in 1967, would be known as Mabou Mines. Another member of the collective was Joanne Akalaitis, who was then Glass's first wife. (Akalaitis went on to become a powerful figure in New York's downtown theatre world, eventually assuming the post of director of the Public Theater.)

Glass soon became an unofficial composer-in-residence for Mabou Mines, and over a period of more more than twenty years wrote a dozen scores for the company. In 1965, however, his music for *Play* came as a shock to all who heard it. 'And no wonder,' wrote Glass. 'Here with *Play*, for instance, was a piece of music based on two lines, each played by soprano saxophone, [each] having only two notes, so that each line represented an alternating, pulsing interval … The result was a very static piece that was still full of rhythmic variety.'

The musicians who heard *Play* were not only surprised; they were downright infuriated. As Glass recalled in 1980:

*At the point where I was really working with repetitive structures and
simple pitch relationships and approached other musicians with it, they
actually became quite angry and wouldn't play it. Originally I was
unprepared for that [anger]. It seemed to me that the music was so simple,
so transparent, what was there to be angry about? Of course, that was
precisely what there was to be angry about. I had, perhaps without
intending it – although that's really hard to know – challenged so many
precepts of the modernist tradition.*

Glass's studies with Boulanger ended in the spring of 1966, without his ever telling her about the renegade musical language he was
beginning to develop. In August 1966, Glass completed a String
Quartet, a work that foreshadows the minimalism that was just
around the corner. The two movements of the Quartet are divided
into a total of thirty-six modules; each module, ranging in length
from seven to ten measures, consists of the repetition of a distinctive
musical phrase. Although the degree of repetition and the static, non-
developmental aura point towards minimalism, the Quartet's chromaticism, dissonance, and elegant counterpoint are very different
from the radically reductive works Glass would begin composing in
New York.

But before Glass and Akalaitis returned to New York, they
explored Asia. The year before, they had taken a side-trip to Morocco,
where Glass (like Riley) had been fascinated by both North African
music and the repetitive, geometric patterns of Islamic art. Now
Shankar inspired them to discover the glories of India. Since 1962
Glass had been practising yoga, but only in 1966 did he begin his
study of Buddhist meditation. (Today he remains a devoted disciple
of Tibetan Buddhism.)

Just before their departure from Paris in the autumn of 1966, Glass
and Akalaitis met Swami Satchidananda, who had an ashram in Sri
Lanka and invited them to study there.

*We went off to India overland, the classic route: through Turkey by
train, through Iran and Afghanistan by bus, into Pakistan through the
Khyber Pass, and then into the Punjab. When I got to New Delhi there
was a letter waiting for me from Swami Satchidananda: 'Dear Student:
You'll be happy to know that I have had a tremendous reception in New*

The Dalai Lama, the spiritual leader of Tibetan Buddhism, of which Glass remains a disciple

York and have started a school here, so there is no reason to go to Ceylon. Please come back to New York. You can study with me here.' Well, I had no intention of returning before seeing India.

So Glass and Akalaitis spent four months travelling, visiting the Himalayan foothills, stopping at various ashrams, finally ending up in Darjeeling. Early in 1967 they arrived in New York – and Glass's official career as a minimalist composer began.

On 18 March 1967, shortly after his return to New York, Glass attended the second of three performances of Steve Reich's music at the Park Place Gallery. Glass had not been in touch with Reich since their days at Juilliard, and he was immensely impressed by the concert, which included a live four-piano version of *Piano Phase*. Afterwards, Glass suggested that they get together so that he could show Reich some of his recent compositions. Reich recalls the meeting:

He showed me his String Quartet, which was the last thing he had written while he was in Europe. It certainly was less dissonant, but it was a piece in transition. I said to him, 'You ought to try to come up with

something that's a little more systematic' – I guess there was a party-line
that we were creating, unbeknownst to ourselves.

And so began one of the great rivalries in contemporary music.
Reich claims that Glass has deliberately obscured the degree to which
his new minimalist language was indebted to Reich. 'In 1967 the giver
was me and the recipient was Glass, and there was a totally dishonest
response,' said Reich bitterly. 'Wittgenstein once said, "Why didn't
Newton acknowledge Leibniz; it would have been such a little thing
to do?" But at the time it must have seemed like an enormous thing
to do. So Glass is in a great tradition of denying influence.' Not only
Reich resents Glass's unwillingness to acknowledge his predecessors.
Even Young speaks sarcastically of him. 'He's not likely to admit
anything,' said Young, more amused than angry. 'He totally came out
of a vacuum; there were no precedents. He knows how he feels about
it, and I'm sure he honestly feels he did. But, knowing that he played
in Steve's group, it seems unlikely.'

Glass, for his part, has said that it is historically simplistic to draw
direct lines of influence, and he has emphasized that there were many
composers working simultaneously to develop a minimalist vocabulary. 'When I came back to New York I would say there were roughly
thirty composers working in a very similar style,' he said in 1988.

If you'll recall that period, it was a very intense generational search –
a lot of people were doing this music. Unfortunately the media has
concentrated on a handful of people and I think it's not been fair – … it
hasn't reflected the variety and vitality of the music that was being done.
And this whole scramble – to be the originator of a style – I think it's silly.

Reich, of course, does not think it is silly, and calls Glass's comments a 'smokescreen' to cover his debt. Certainly some of the irrita-
tion Reich and Young display is due simply to their jealousy of Glass's
greater commercial success. Ultimately, however, the proof lies in
the music. And its chronology would seem to support Reich's point
of view.

Immediately after his return to New York, Glass radically
simplified his musical style, and to a degree unparalleled in any of
his Parisian works. The chromaticism and dissonance of the String

Quartet was rejected in favour of a plain, consonant vocabulary; the intertwining counterpoint was replaced by unison or parallel textures; the tempos turned rapid and the dynamics loud. And now Glass developed a systematic approach to composition – but instead of using Reich's phasing technique, Glass came up with an original musical process based on the additive rhythmic structure he had learned from Indian music.

The first step along this path was *Strung Out* (1967) for solo amplified violin, which consists merely of a steady stream of rapid, unbarred eighth notes. Employing only five pitches, the constant repetition proceeds by means of Glass's trademark additive process. A similar method is used in *1+1* (1968), for one person tapping on an amplified table-top. Almost as spartan is *Two Pages* (1968), in which a single musical line, played by unison electric keyboards and winds, elongates or contracts in length. (In an act of homage, Glass originally titled the work *Two Pages for Steve Reich*; by 1969 it was shortened, without comment, to *Two Pages*.)

How does Glass's additive (and subtractive) process work? As a musical module is repeated, it expands or shrinks in length. (*Two Pages*, for instance, possesses 107 such modules, each repeated an indefinite number of times.) If the module consists of four pitches and a fifth is suddenly added, that new five-note configuration will be repeated; if, conversely, the module consists of four pitches and one is suddenly subtracted, that new three-note configuration will be repeated. But since the rhythm, typically a rapid torrent of eighth notes, never changes, and since the dynamic is unremittingly loud, the texture is an unadorned unison, and there is no harmony to speak of, these early works of Glass are more radical than any minimalist music to date.

Glass and Reich pooled their resources, and for the first few years of their relationship they actually shared the same band. (The nucleus of that ensemble was the group that had been performing with Reich since 1966.) Soon Glass and Reich each gave a concert at the Film-Makers Cinematheque in Soho; Glass's evening, on 19 May 1968, marked the first New York concert devoted entirely to his music. The programme included *Strung Out*, the music of which was, according to Glass, literally 'tacked onto the wall, running about fifteen feet before taking a right turn out from the wall and forming an L-shape.'

Dorothy Pixley-Rothschild
performs Glass's *Strung
Out,* the score of which is
tacked to the wall; these
pictures were taken at the
Film-Makers Cinematheque
in New York, 1968.

Also performed was *Music in the Form of a Square* (an allusion to Erik Satie's *Music in the Shape of a Pear*), a piece set up in a big square, each side of which was ten feet long. Glass and Jon Gibson both played flutes: 'We began to play, walking in opposite directions around the square, and we came to the end of the piece at our starting point.' Summarizing the evening, Glass wrote that 'it was a very conceptual concert. A very *neat* concert. And it was both visual and musical. The audience was mostly artists, about 120 people, which in the little Film-Makers Cinematheque made the place seem *packed*.'

Like Reich, Glass performed in his ensemble, partly out of necessity (since no mainstream organization would touch his music) and partly out of principle. The ideal of a composer playing his own music with his own band is unusual in the classical world but commonplace in rock, and indeed the strident sound of Glass's ensemble already was very different from the gentle amplification of Reich's musicians. Consisting primarily of portable, rock-style electric organs and amplified winds, Glass's virtuoso band was a blistering whirlwind in perpetual motion.

Unlike Reich, Riley and Young, who were strongly influenced by jazz, Glass was always much closer to rock. It is no coincidence that he frequently played in rock clubs, that he went on to influence rock musicians such as David Bowie and Brian Eno, that he would later collaborate (in *Songs from Liquid Days* of 1985) with pop artists such as David Byrne and Paul Simon, and that in the early 1980s he even produced a rock band, Polyrock. Although Glass's ensemble didn't include percussion, the pulsating rhythms, the relentless repetition, the deafening volume and the electric keyboards all reinforced a kinship with rock that certainly propelled his commercial success in the popular-music world.

In the meantime, however, commercial success was still far off. Not only were Glass and Reich the sole employees of Chelsea Light Moving, but Glass also worked as a plumber. Later he described a day when he went 'to install a dishwasher in a loft in Soho. While working, I suddenly heard a noise and looked up to find Robert Hughes, the art critic of *Time* Magazine, staring at me in disbelief. "But you're Philip Glass! What are you doing here?" It was obvious that I was installing his dishwasher, and I told him I soon would be finished. (I have always been careful about deadlines.)

"But you are an artist," he protested. "I won't permit you to work on my dishwasher."'

During 1969 and 1970, Glass and Reich found that the joint engagements for their still-unified (and as yet unnamed) ensemble were increasing. Most of these were in unorthodox locations, whether a downtown venue like The New School, or uptown museums like the Whitney and the Guggenheim. (Not until after their first European tour of 1971 would the band split into the Philip Glass Ensemble and Steve Reich and Musicians.) At these New York concerts, Glass performed the works he had composed in 1969 and 1970 – a group of minimalist masterpieces, as shocking in their reductive audacity and exhilarating in their propulsive drive as anything ever penned.

Music in Fifths (1969), for instance, consists of two lines of unceasing, rapid-fire eighth notes; each line expands and contracts by means of the additive/subtractive process, and the two run continuously in nakedly exposed parallel fifths. (The critic Tim Page remarked that 'Glass has always considered *Music in Fifths* a sort of teasing homage to Boulanger; it is written entirely in parallel fifths, a cardinal sin in the traditional counterpoint his teacher so carefully instructed.') *Music in Contrary Motion* (1969) is made up of two torrential lines of eighth notes, each elongating and contracting, but the two now move in contrary rather than parallel motion; beneath them, a bass is added as a drone. *Music in Similar Motion* (1969) thickens the texture even further, beginning with one line of unison eighth notes and expanding to four simultaneous parts, all moving in similar motion.

Even today, Glass's early works seem like a veritable minimalist manifesto. Certainly they are as shockingly stark and formally rigorous as any solid black canvas. None of these pieces have any changes in instrumentation, rhythm, tempo or dynamics; all reject the goal-oriented, developmental model of Western music; all favour a non-directional steady-state that suspends the passage of time.

It is all too easy to dismiss Glass's early compositions as simple-minded repetition. But they are not quite as simple as they seem. At first the relentless repetition can seem merely hypnotic. Listen carefully, however, and you begin to notice a wealth of subtly shifting detail. Soon you realize that hardly any repetition is literal – that although the slamming pulse remains steady, the whirling melodies are constantly changing in length and the colours are dancing like a ghostly aurora. Like some ecstatic devotional ritual, the music aims to transcend, to open the mind to new states of consciousness. Although it can be listened to for its mesmerizing, drug-like effect, its real value is in heightening awareness, not numbing it.

In *Music with Changing Parts* (1970) Glass took his additive process and expanded it to epic proportions. (Since the number of repetitions is not specified, *Music with Changing Parts* can vary in length from one to two hours.) For the first and last time, Glass allowed a small amount of carefully controlled improvisation, such as the addition of drone-like sustained tones in the winds and voices. When Glass took *Music with Changing Parts* to England in March 1971, both David Bowie and Brian Eno heard a performance of it at the Royal College of Art in London. It is not coincidental that both the drones and the rapid, pulsating repetition quickly showed up in their work.

But Glass was not thrilled with the improvisatory element in *Music with Changing Parts*. 'It was a little too spacey for my tastes,' he said in 1993. 'We don't play it much anymore. But it was very important to my development. I proved to myself that the music I was making could sustain attention over a prolonged period of time – an hour or more. And that led directly to *Music in Twelve Parts* and then on to the operas.'

By the early 1970s the Philip Glass Ensemble had become standardized as a group of electric keyboards (with Glass himself playing one), some amplified woodwinds, and a couple of female voices who sang a textless vocalise. Joining them was sound designer Kurt Munkacsi (today Glass's producer) and, a bit later, music director Michael Riesman.

Thanks to Munkacsi's connnections, Glass was able to launch his own record company, Chatham Square Productions. Chatham Square was designed, according to Glass, 'for the purpose of making my music more widely available since no commercial record company would touch it at the time.' The limited-edition double-album of *Music with Changing Parts* that Chatham Square released in 1971 would later became a cult item. Recorded in a single weekend in 1971, it preserves the sound of the Philip Glass Ensemble at its most raucous and elated.

The ensemble, with its long hair, scruffy clothes, and assault-style amplification, soon developed an enthusiastic young audience that followed it to universities, museums, galleries, and underground rock clubs. But Glass's performances were certainly not lacking in controversy. In 1970 Glass went to Europe for the first time, as an assistant to the minimalist sculptor Richard Serra. During an Amsterdam performance of his keyboard music, a member of the audience leaped onstage and tried to play along. Glass, a former wrestler, punched him with one hand and kept playing with the other. 'I punched him – of which I'm not proud. I didn't get him really good but enough to knock him off the stage.' In 1972 at the Spoleto Festival in Italy, the festival's director, composer Gian Carlo Menotti, walked out during the performance, and someone else tried to cut the power supply. At an outdoor concert in New York in 1973, there was some additional excitement: 'A man literally tried to stop the concert by yelling, "They're not musicians! They can't play! I'm a music teacher and I know they're not really playing their instruments!"'

Still, there was always the faithful downtown visual-arts crowd to fall back on for support. One evening in the spring of 1973, the Philip Glass Ensemble played *Music with Changing Parts*, in a ninety-minute incarnation, at the Soho loft of the minimalist sculptor Donald Judd. John Rockwell, the *New York Times* music critic most sympathetic to minimalism, described the event in enraptured terms:

Glass's ensemble that night played with the spirit and precision that only years together can bring. The music danced and pulsed with a special life, its motoric rhythms, burbling, highly amplified figurations, and mournful sustained notes booming out through the huge black windows and filling up the bleak industrial neighborhood. It was so loud that the dancers Douglas Dunn and Sara Rudner, who were strolling down Wooster Street, sat on a stoop and enjoyed the concert together from afar. A pack of teenagers kept up an ecstatic dance of their own. And across the street, silhouetted high up in a window, a lone saxophone player improvised in silent accompaniment like some faded postcard of Greenwich Village Bohemia. It was a good night to be in New York City.

On 1 June 1974 Glass made his first trip uptown to a conventional concert venue, Town Hall. The event was a remarkable success: 1200 of the 1400 seats were filled, the audience gave Glass a standing ovation, and the more open-minded critics began to grant him a certain

Philip Glass performed in
the Soho loft of the
minimalist sculptor Donald
Judd. Judd's work, here
represented by *Untitled*
(1965), often took the form
of repeated shapes.

grudging acceptance. The composition that Glass chose for his uptown debut was his magnum opus, *Music in Twelve Parts* – a work he had been composing continuously from 1971 to 1974, and a landmark in his creative output. *Music in Twelve Parts* is roughly parallel to Reich's *Music for 18 Musicians*, for both pieces mark a turn away from the austere, severly reductive minimalism that the two composers had pioneered just a few years earlier.

Music in Twelve Parts is a punning title. On the one hand, the work is scored for twelve musical lines (two each for the three electric keyboards, and six for amplified winds and, occasionally, a soprano). On the other hand, the work consists of twelve sections, each about twenty minutes in length. A complete performance typically took nearly five and a half hours – including a one-hour dinner break.

Glass has said that he intended *Music in Twelve Parts* to be a summation of all his minimalist techniques to date, and he was not joking. (The critic Tim Page has called *Music in Twelve Parts* Glass's 'Art of Repetition', intending to draw a parallel with Bach's summation of fugal technique, 'The Art of the Fugue'.) Some of the twelve movements are interconnected, others are free-standing; some hark back to the unison writing of his first minimalist pieces, others are laid out in dense, intertwining counterpoint; some use an additive process, others turn to more traditional Western ideas of augmentation and diminution. Some of the movements are as static and unvarying as any of Glass's early works. But in others Glass explores new techniques – especially in the realm of harmony.

The latter sections of *Music in Twelve Parts* turn to an increasingly varied and directionalized harmonic language, including modulation to remote keys and a slinky, unpredictable sort of chromaticism. In Part 12, the bass-line grows by additive means from a brief cadential progression to a chromatic scale that embraces all twelve tones – perhaps Glass's impudent homage to serialism. John Rockwell wrote that Part 12 'suddenly erupted into functional, root-movement harmony – in other words, full-fledged tonality. From there, the way was open to the large-scale tonal organization conducive to opera.'

Just as the dense textures, lush instrumentation, and harmonic motion of Reich's *Music for 18 Musicians* had rendered the question of musical process irrelevant, so too did *Music in Twelve Parts* suggest that the term minimalism had outlived its usefulness. Glass himself has long insisted that 'for me minimalism was over by 1974.' In 1988, he explained why: 'Because from that point on I was engaged almost entirely with working in theatre. I'd always worked in theatre with Mabou Mines, but at that point it became almost entirely my line of work, and my feeling was that the aesthetic of the theatre is additive rather than reductive, which in this context is almost counterproductive or counterindicated.'

In other words, Glass felt that the demands of music-theatre and the austerity of minimalism were mutually exclusive. Within just a few years, he would demonstrate his newly maximalist tendencies in *Einstein on the Beach* (1976) – his first opera, one of his greatest achievements, and a turning point in the history of American theatre.

5

A mature Philip Glass,
posed for a formal portrait

[Jean Cocteau's] film Orphée *is an autobiographical work about an older artist displaced
by a younger one. And whom is he killed by at
the end? His fellow poets. When Orphée asserts
to the critic that he's adored by the public,
the critic says, 'but the public is alone.' A
wonderful line.*

Philip Glass, 1994

Philip Glass, Maximalist

Beginning with *Einstein on the Beach*, Glass's career turned irrevocably toward opera and music-theatre. And so great has been his success that he has ended up playing a decisive role in the revitalization of American opera – for by the 1970s the genre seemed stale, moribund, and practically beyond hope of resuscitation.

Glass's collaborator in *Einstein on the Beach* was Robert Wilson, the visionary American stage director whose work had become known for its striking imagery, epic proportions, and cryptic, non-narrative approach to meaning. All these elements were perfectly suited to Glass's similarly non-developmental, time-suspending music.

Glass and Wilson began meeting regularly in the spring of 1974. They were occasionally joined by Christopher Knowles, at the time a fourteen-year-old autistic boy who possessed, in Glass's words, a 'strikingly unusual way of viewing the world.' Both Glass and Wilson were interested in basing their opera on a historical figure: Wilson had already created the all-night theatre piece *The Life and Times of Joseph Stalin* (1973), and he now proposed Chaplin or Hitler as possible subjects. Glass preferred Gandhi (who would eventually become the centerpiece of his second opera, *Satyagraha*). And Wilson finally suggested Einstein, who appealed to Glass – since the scientist was also a passionate amateur violinist.

Next, Glass and Wilson designed the overall shape of *Einstein*. They settled on a time-frame of four hours (it ended up being closer to five), three enigmatic visual themes (train, trial-with-bed, field-with-spaceship), an Einstein character who would have ample opportunity to play the violin, and a four-act structure linked together by 'knee-plays' – interludes with a connective function akin to the human knee. Everyone onstage would sport an Einstein costume of baggy pants, suspenders, short-sleeved shirt, and pipe. All the visual elements, including trains, rockets, gyroscopes and clocks, would be associated with Einstein and his scientific discoveries. And everything would unfold in one vast expanse of music and theatre.

Robert Wilson's original
title-page drawing for the
1976 opera *Einstein on the
Beach*; the work marked a
turning point in the history of
American music-theatre

But *Einstein on the Beach* would go even further in shattering the
rules of traditional opera. Its nearly five hours of music proceeded
without an intermission; audience members were free to come and go
as they chose. It lacked any formal libretto, and its sung texts consisted only of numbers and solfège syllables (do, re, mi) that reflected,
respectively, the rhythmic and melodic structure of the music. Its
other texts, which were spoken, featured some disarmingly elusive
poems by Knowles, the choreographer Lucinda Childs and the actor
Samuel M. Johnson. Instead of a symphony orchestra and
operatically trained singers, *Einstein* used the Philip Glass Ensemble (a
highly-amplified blend of two electric organs, three woodwinds, a
female voice and a solo violin) to accompany a group of untrained
vocalists who were called upon to sing, act, and dance in equal
measure.

Since there would be neither character development nor conventional narrative, *Einstein* would be given shape by means of its continuous music and its recurring visual images. But what did those images
symbolize? Clearly, Glass and Wilson were attempting to create a
prismatic, metaphorical view of Einstein – a musician, scientist, and
humanist who, ironically enough, made nuclear annihilation a real
possibility. Perhaps, then, the trains referred back to a pre-atomic era;
the trial that occurred over and over was an indictment of science
itself; the bed was symbolic of Einstein's dream-like, metaphysical
side; and the spaceship suggested science's more constructive purposes.
Certainly there was no doubt that the penultimate scene warned of
a nuclear holocaust wrought by science run amok.

Following page, the
spaceship scene from Philip
Glass and Robert Wilson's
landmark music-theatre
work, *Einstein on the Beach*,
as it was conceived at the
Brooklyn Academy of Music
revival in 1984

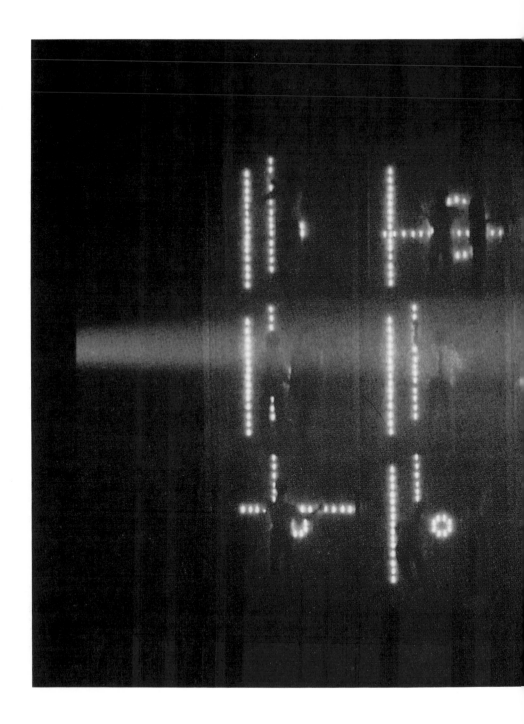

Glass and Wilson have spent nearly twenty years trying to explain their most famous work – or, perhaps, insisting that it needs no explanation. 'It never occurred to us that *Einstein on the Beach* would have a story or contain anything like an ordinary plot,' Glass wrote in 1987. 'I saw *Einstein on the Beach* more as a portrait opera. In this case the portrait of Einstein that we would be constructing replaced the idea of plot, narrative, development, all the paraphenalia of conventional theater. Furthermore, we understood that this portrait of Einstein was a poetic vision.' Ultimately, Glass admitted: 'It hardly mattered what you thought *Einstein on the Beach* might "mean" … In the case of *Einstein on the Beach*, the story was supplied by the imaginations of the audience, and there was no way for us to predict, even if we wanted to, what the story might be for any particular person.'

In 1984, at the time of *Einstein*'s first American revival, Wilson claimed that the lack of narrative served to free the viewer.

Ours is the easiest of all operas. You don't have to think about the story, because there isn't any. You don't have to listen to the words, because they don't mean anything. I'm not giving you puzzles to solve, only pictures to hear. You go to our opera like you go to a museum. You appreciate the color of the apple, the line of the dress, the glow of the light. You go to the park, you look at the scenery which contains people moving about and sounds changing. Watch clouds passing. Look at the music. Listen to the pictures.

Opposite, Philip Glass and Robert Wilson take a break during rehearsals for *Einstein on the Beach*, 1976.

To anyone who has ever experienced *Einstein*, the question of meaning seems beside the point. What sticks in the memory are the achingly beautiful visual tableaux, each unfolding at a glacial pace, each created in part by a breathtaking use of light. During one of the trial scenes, the bed, which has always been a huge, monolithic presence, begins slowly, magically, to rise. Demarcated by a single fluorescent tube attached to its length, the bed is at first a horizontal slab of light; it takes more than twenty minutes for it to tilt to a vertical bar and finally ascend from the stage.

Complementing such slowly unfolding imagery is Glass's music, which displays many of the reductive qualities of his earlier minimalism but also ranges over a wider variety of moods and techniques. There are the familiar hyperactive eighth-note lines that expand and

The Metropolitan Opera, New York, where *Einstein on the Beach* received its American première in November 1976

contract by means of an additive process, but there are also calmer, more incantatory sections, such as when the chorus ritualistically chants the numbers and solfège syllables. And there is a new fascination with the power of harmonic motion to shape and unify a large-scale structure.

Glass completed the music to *Einstein* by November 1975, and the following months were spent in gruelling, six-day-a-week rehearsals. During the rehearsal process the music continued to evolve. Glass initially used the solfège syllables and numbers merely as an aid in memorization, and only later made them the text of the choral parts. Similarly, he decided for practical reasons to leave the poetic commentary as spoken material. 'For me, the main problem was that I had had very little experience in recent years setting words to music,' he wrote. 'As a student, I had written quite a lot of vocal and choral music, but that had been more than fourteen years earlier. Finally I suggested we use the text as a spoken part over the music.'

In August 1976 *Einstein on the Beach* received its world première at the Avignon Festival in France, and it quickly gained a cult following. After touring five more European countries, *Einstein* came to New York in November 1976. Instead of being staged at an alternative performance space, *Einstein* received its American première in the hallowed hall of the Metropolitan Opera – which was dark and empty each Sunday night, and could be rented for such special events.

Word of *Einstein*'s spectacular success had reached New York from Europe, and Glass, who had never played to an American audience larger than that of Town Hall, was suddenly faced with a sold-out Metropolitan Opera House. A second performance was added for the following Sunday night, and that quickly sold out too. Some of those in the audience were traditionalists who stormed out noisily – and gave their ticket stubs to the throngs outside eager to get in. Others were curious trend-spotters, intrigued by the growing legend of Glass but uninitiated into the rites of opera. Glass recalls:

For many who were there on those two evenings, it no doubt was their first time in an opera house anywhere. I remember standing backstage during the second Sunday's performance, watching the audience with one of the higher-up administrators of the Metropolitan Opera. He asked me 'Who are these people? I've never seen them here before.' I remember replying very candidly, 'Well, you'd better find out who they are, because if this place expects to be running in twenty-five years, that's your audience out there.'

Glass didn't know it then, but it would not take twenty-five years to recapture that audience. Sixteen years later Glass's opera *The Voyage* (1992) was presented in the same hall – only this time the work was commissioned and given its first performance by the Metropolitan Opera. Glass, once the scruffy rebel, was now a darling of the establishment.

In the meantime, however, there were bills to pay. *Einstein*'s year-long tab came to $900,000, of which $90,000 was still outstanding. In addition, each sold-out performance at the Met actually lost $10,000, which accounted for the fact that no further Sunday nights were planned. The 'Einstein debt', as it was soon known, became legendary in the downtown arts world. Wilson sold his drawings, Glass sold his score, and their fellow artists organized benefits and auctions. A commercial recording might have raised money, but no label would touch what would have been a five-LP set. (Later, in 1978, Tomato Records released an abbreviated *Einstein* on four LPs, and the set went on to sell more than 20,000 copies.)

For the first time in his career Glass was a celebrity, yet outwardly his life was unchanged. 'I returned to making my living by driving a cab, as I had during most of the 1970s, and I vividly remember the moment, shortly after the Met adventure, when a well-dressed woman got into my cab. After noting the name of the driver … , she leaned forward and said: "Young man, do you realize you have the same name as a very famous composer?"'

It would have been more accurate to describe him as a very famous *opera* composer, because *Einstein* had whetted Glass's appetite for music-theatre like nothing he had done in the past. Now he began to see *Einstein* as merely the first instalment in what would become a trilogy of 'portrait operas' – each one looking at a seminal figure in a different field of human endeavour. *Einstein*, clearly, had looked at the realm of science. *Satyagraha* (1979), his next opera, would focus on the figure of Gandhi and examine the realm of politics. And *Akhnaten* (1983) would use its title character, an ancient Egyptian pharaoh, to investigate the realm of religion.

Despite *Einstein*'s success, no American company was eager to commission Glass's second opera; in fact, Glass approached the Metropolitan Opera and the New York City Opera, and both turned him down. It was left to the Dutch to come to the rescue. Shortly after the Amsterdam performance of *Einstein*, Glass was invited to visit Hans de Roo, the director of the Netherlands Opera. Glass recounted their post-*Einstein* conversation: '"Well, Philip, that was very interesting. Now, how would you like to write a *real* opera?" What did he mean by a real opera? "It should be for my orchestra, chorus and soloists, people trained and practiced in the singing of traditional operas."' At first Glass had his doubts, since he felt that the radical *Einstein* – lacking narrative, orchestra, and operatic voices – wasn't really an opera. And, he added, 'the operatic tradition seemed to me hopelessly dead, with no prospect for resurrection in the world of performance in which I worked.'

Soon, however, he was won over by the idea of framing his musical language in a more conventionally operatic context. The City of Rotterdam, where the Netherlands Opera was to present the première, came up with a $20,000 commission, and Glass quickly went to work. He had no hesitation in proposing a subject: Gandhi, a man who had not thrilled Wilson three years earlier, but who continued to fascinate Glass. Rather than attempting an epic narrative that would encapsulate Gandhi's entire life, Glass wisely decided to focus on a

single, formative period in his career. That was his sojourn in South
Africa, the period from 1893 to 1914 when his political philosophy of
non-violent resistance – what he called 'satyagraha', or 'truth-force' –
was formulated.

The opera, too, was to be called *Satyagraha*. In the winter of 1978
Glass, along with his librettist Constance De Jong and his designer
Robert Israel, travelled to India. They visited Gandhi's last ashram,
dug through the archives of the Gandhi Peace Foundation, and witnessed the multi-media religious pageantry of Khatikali music-theatre.
When they returned to New York in early 1979, they were ready to
frame their work in concrete terms.

Gandhi's South African years, in which he united the expatriate
Indian community by carrying out acts of civil disobedience against
the British, offered an overabundance of incidents that seemed ideal
for the stage. Glass and De Jong whittled these down to six vivid
episodes: the founding of Gandhi's ashram, Tolstoy Farm; the vow to
resist the Government's imposition of registration cards; the attack
on Gandhi by a white mob; the establishment of a newspaper, *Indian
Opinion*; the burning of registration cards; and the historic non-
violent Newcastle March.

Clearly these were isolated chunks of narrative, as discontinuous
(if not as elusive) as anything in *Einstein*. How might they be unified?
First, Glass and De Jong sought to frame them, theatrically speaking,
within the span of a single day, from dawn to dusk. Second, they
took the six scenes and divided them into three hour-long acts – each
witnessed by a silent figure, a personification of satyagraha, who
hovers high above the stage. Act I is watched over by Leo Tolstoy; Act
II by the Indian writer Rabindranath Tagore; and Act III by Martin
Luther King.

Before the musical composition could proceed, there was the not
insignificant question of the libretto to be resolved. Glass still had no
interest in setting a straightforward, narrative libretto, and De Jong
was not eager to write one. So they turned to the great Hindu religious epic, the *Bhagavad-Gita*. De Jong, rather than putting words in
the mouths of the characters, chose extracts from the *Gita* that suggested the philosophical basis for personal action. In fact, a scene from
the *Gita* – the battlefield meeting of Prince Arjuna and Lord Krishna,
in which they speak of the moral justification for political resistance –

Philip Glass's *Satyagraha*, as it was restaged by director Achim Freyer for Stuttgart Opera; Act II, scene II shows the production of Gandhi's newspaper *Indian Opinion*.

was added as a prelude, just as many Baroque operas open with an allegorical scene that reveals the work's moral.

In what language would this libretto be cast? The *Bhagavad-Gita*, after all, is in Sanskrit, a tongue nearly as dead as Latin, and one that might seem pretentious and absurd to Western audiences. But since the libretto itself was merely commentary – it neither engendered action nor suggested character development – there was no real need to make it understood. So it remained in Sanskrit, a mellifluous language that turned out to be graceful to sing. 'At first the decision troubled me, but more and more, I found it appealing,' wrote Glass. 'I liked the idea of *further* separating the vocal text from the action. In this way, without an understandable text to contend with, the listener could let the words go altogether. The weight of "meaning" would then be thrown onto the music, the designs, and the stage action.'

With De Jong's Sanskrit extracts from the *Gita* now at hand, Glass could get down to composing. Apparently the process was an easy one, because by August 1979 the opera was not only complete but fully orchestrated. (In fact, Glass had composed directly into orchestral score; a piano reduction had to be made later.) Considering the special musical challenges that *Satyagraha* posed, his facility is all the more remarkable.

The first problem was the orchestra – no longer the Philip Glass Ensemble, but a real symphonic pit orchestra. Glass had not written for such an instrumental body since his days in the Pittsburgh public schools, some fifteen years earlier. 'In thinking about the orchestra for *Satyagraha*, I saw that the solution lay precisely in thinking of orchestral writing in the same way that I had thought of writing for my own Ensemble,' he wrote. 'The sound would be based on that of my own Ensemble, which was, up to that point, a sound I had made my own. What better model could I find than the one which had served my purposes so well until then?'

So Glass scored *Satyagraha* for an unusual fifty-one-piece orchestra, rich in strings and winds (three each of flutes, clarinets, oboes, and bassoons) but devoid of brass or percussion. (One electric organ would serve as a literal reminder of his own Ensemble.) This orchestration lends *Satyagraha* its special timbre – plangent, reedy, and, unlike Glass's own Ensemble, never harsh or strident. Indeed, the mellow, blended sound seems to reflect the dignity and repose with which Gandhi's philosophy of satyagraha unfolds.

The second problem was the vocal writing. It was not the chorus that concerned Glass, who had spent his teenage years singing choral music. The forty-member chorus, in fact, is the veritable star of *Satyagraha*, appearing in four of its seven scenes and making the work practically an opera-oratorio.

Of much greater concern were the solo vocal lines. Conservative in their narrow range and avoidance of operatic display, they are demanding only in the amount of mental concentration they require; it cannot be easy to keep track of numerous repetitions, especially when you have had to memorize a text in Sanskrit. Glass claimed that the vocal parts and ensembles – from duets to sextets – came to him easily. And no one can dispute the gracefulness of the vocal melodies, which soar luminously above the orchestra and chorus.

But in *Satyagraha* a problematic aspect of Glass's vocal writing begins to emerge. Although the rapid instrumental lines display their typical rhythmic ingenuity, the slow-moving vocal parts are four-square and sing-song in their declamation. In Sanskrit, it hardly matters. In English such wooden, predictable scansion would prove to be far more troubling.

English, however, was still years away. In the meantime, Glass created a score for *Satyagraha* that he has never surpassed. Each of the seven scenes is cast as a *passacaglia*, a Baroque variation form in which the bass-line remains constant, but the melody above changes. Act I, Scene I, for instance, is built upon 143 repetitions of a four-chord progression, each iteration overlaid with a new vocal melody. Even more single-minded is Gandhi's last aria, which consists of a rising scale from E to E sung thirty times, while a three-chord progression is repeated beneath. Far from being simplistic, these structures are used with an ingenuity worthy of Henry Purcell, and although there might appear to be much repetition, hardly any of it is literal.

Satyagraha received its première in Rotterdam in September 1980, and came to America in the summer of 1981. Most critics seemed to realize that it was a very special opera, far more Glass's own conception than *Einstein* had been. With its delicate, understated timbres, its sober, extended vocal writing, and its exquisitely formalistic structure, it projected a high moral bearing worthy of its subject. Indeed some critics pointed out that *Satyagraha* was a modern-day counterpart to Wagner's *Parsifal*, more of a religious mystery-play or pageant than an opera.

Satyagraha has no real narrative to speak of, although the events
it traces are easily comprehended; it has no interest in character development; and, despite its subject, it conveys little conflict or drama.
Instead, it is a series of introspective, contemplative tableaux, each
a serene meditation on the theme of non-violence. By the time the
radiance of dawn turned to the star-filled sky of dusk, *Satyagraha's*
ecstatic lyricism and luminous textures had converted most of the
sceptics in the audience. Philip Glass could write a *real* opera after all.

Glass's achievement was all the more significant precisely because
Satyagraha had been written for an opera house, not for the world
of experimental music-theatre. *Satyagraha* suggested that American
opera could be rejuvenated, perhaps by taking a contemporary subject
but clothing it in traditional vocal and instrumental garb. Without
Satyagraha, it is unlikely that Anthony Davis would have composed
X: The Life and Times of Malcolm X (1986) – or John Adams written
Nixon in China (1987).

But this embrace of tradition came at a price. *Einstein* had represented a genuine rethinking of what opera could mean for the modern
age. With *Satyagraha*, however, Glass began a long, gradual march
back toward convention. Never again would he write music of the
audacity and reductive force of his works of the 1960s and 70s. Never
again, in fact, could the word minimalism be used with any accuracy
to refer to his music. Throughout the 1980s, Glass would slowly and
steadily re-embrace much of the harmonic and melodic language
he had previously shunned, until by the end of the decade his once
austere minimalism would project an almost neo-Romantic expressive
force. Whether this broadening of his musical vocabulary has
enhanced the stature of his work has been a matter for debate. But
after *Satyagraha*, there could be no doubting Glass's desire to court
the mainstream.

Glass's hard-core fans, who loved his strident rock-influenced
minimalism, may have been turned off by the subtleties of *Satyagraha*.
But now he was winning new audiences of a size and diversity nearly
unknown to late-twentieth-century composers. The *Village Voice's*
critic Gregory Sandow, who reviewed the 1981 Brooklyn Academy of
Music performance of *Satyagraha*, posed a rhetorical question that
captured the social significance of Glass's new public: 'When a work
of the highest artistic and moral stature comes along that's in many

ways modern and severe, and even so plays to sold-out houses and standing ovations, drawing audiences who rarely think about classical music, shouldn't the music world ask what's going on?'

Indeed, it did. This time it did not prove very difficult to gain a commission for the third opera in Glass's trilogy, *Akhnaten.* In 1981 the Stuttgart State Opera (under its American music director, Dennis Russell Davies) presented *Satyagraha* in a new version directed by Achim Freyer, and shortly thereafter the company decided to commission *Akhnaten.* The idea was to bring together all three operas, in three new productions by Freyer, as a sort of Glassian 'Ring' cycle. (That feat was achieved in June 1990, when the operas were performed, twice, as a successive three-evening cycle – and all played to sold-out houses.)

Glass knew that his trilogy would have to be capped with a historical figure worthy of Gandhi and Einstein, and his search for a successor led him in an unlikely direction. It was in ancient Egypt that Glass found his subject. Akhnaten, who lived from 1385 to 1357 BC, was an Egyptian pharaoh whose brief seventeen-year reign was cut short by a combined military and religious coup. Upon assuming power,

Philip Glass looks over the score of *Akhnaten*, the third opera of his trilogy – perhaps the most important operatic cycle since Wagner's *Ring.*

Akhnaten had deposed Egypt's pantheon of gods and replaced them with a new religion, one that focused on the single deity of Aten. Aten, who was associated with the sun, was an abstract god-head, and Akhnaten, by introducing him, became the world's first monotheist. But the Egyptian people, the priesthood, and the military rebelled against this radically new notion, and soon Akhnaten was overthrown and the old religious order restored.

Akhnaten has long fascinated philosophers and historians, who wonder if his ideas may have inspired the monotheism of the ancient Hebrews. For Glass, Akhnaten provided a satisfying completion for his trilogy. 'First of all, Akhnaten, like Einstein and Gandhi, had changed forever the world into which he was born,' wrote Glass. 'But the main point for me was that Akhnaten had changed his (and our) world through the force of his ideas and not through the force of arms.' With Akhnaten, Glass now complemented his man of Science and his man of Politics with a man of Religion.

Early in his work on *Akhnaten*, Glass went to Egypt, just as he had once gone to India to research *Satyagraha*. He visited the Cairo Musuem (which has a room devoted to Akhnaten), Luxor (the site of Egypt's ancient capital), and Tell El-Amarna, where the ruins of Akhnaten's city, Akhetaten, are crumbling in the desert sands. And he realized that although it would prove impossible to flesh out the full story of Akhnaten's life, numerous tantalizing fragments survived – documentation of his marriage to Nefertiti; a statement of his religious philosophy; and the physical evidence, in the form of sculpture, of his shocking appearance. Art of Akhnaten's period, Glass discovered, showed him to be an 'odd-looking character' with 'swollen thighs, enlarged hips, breasts almost pendulous. At first glance he appears almost hermaphroditic.' These fragments of Akhnaten's life would prove sufficient to create a typically Glassian scenario, one stitched together from discrete, symbolic episodes. 'It seemed to me … that we needed no more story than was already there, that the missing pieces, far from needing to be filled in or explained, actually added to the mystery and beauty of our subject,' he wrote.

With the help of Shalom Goldman, a professor of Near Eastern history at New York University, Glass assembled texts related to Akhnaten's stormy reign. In the end, the development of the libretto resembled the process of selecting excerpts from the *Bhagavad-Gita*.

Opposite, the Pharaoh Akhnaten (played by Christopher Robson) and Queen Nefertiti (Sally Burgess) in the English National Opera's 1985 production of Glass's opera *Akhnaten*

Scenes from Philip Glass's *Akhnaten*, an opera which traces the rise and fall of the ancient Egyptian Pharaoh, one of the world's first monotheists

Most of the texts in *Akhnaten* would come from the Pharaoh's own time, and nearly all would be sung in their original language, whether Egyptian, Akkadian or Hebrew. Considering that Glass had just set an opera in Sanskrit, the use of exotic and ancient tongues hardly seemed surprising. But Glass, in a gesture to his increasingly mainstream public, rendered the libretto comprehensible by including a narrator, whose job it is to speak the entire text, over accompanying music, in the language of the audience.

Akhnaten, like *Satyagraha*, falls into three acts. The first, full of regal pomp and splendour, shows the funeral of Akhnaten's father, Amenhotep III, and his son's coronation. The second documents the establishment of Akhnaten's new religion and ends with his credo (and the only surviving text he authored), the 'Hymn to the Sun'. And the third traces his downfall and eventual overthrow. It ends with the opera's only serious miscalculation – a jarring and unintentionally comic Epilogue set in present-day Egypt, in which a group of bored, garishly dressed tourists are guided through the ruins of Akhetaten.

Musically, *Akhnaten* goes beyond *Satyagraha* in moving even further away from Glass's minimalist origins. The orchestra is an unusual one, with winds, brass and a large complement of percussion, but no violins; the absence of upper strings creates an ominous, brooding sound ideally suited to the tragic subject. Throughout, the orchestra is used more colourfully and more soloistically than in *Satyagraha*. A solo trumpet, for instance, is associated with Akhnaten, and accompanies the Pharaoh whenever he takes centre-stage. And the exoticism and sheer violence of Glass's orchestra become obvious already in Act I, when Amenhotep's funeral calls forth ceremonial music of brutal force.

Most remarkable is the character of Akhnaten himself. Glass searched for a way to depict, in musical terms, the freakish, nearly other-worldly quality of Akhnaten's physical appearance, and in the end he decided to cast him as a countertenor. 'The effect of hearing a high, beautiful voice coming from the lips of a full-grown man can at first be very startling,' he wrote. 'In one stroke, Akhnaten would be separated from everyone around him.'

Nowhere does this strategy work more effectively than in the ecstatic 'Hymn to the Sun', Akhnaten's statement of belief and the opera's high point. The radiant countertenor intertwines with the solo trumpet and floats high above the orchestra, just as Gandhi's tenor had shimmered above its instrumental ensemble. After Akhnaten concludes his song of praise, an offstage chorus softly sings Psalm 104 in Hebrew – a dramatic stroke both brilliantly effective and historically revealing, for the Biblical Psalm shares imagery with Akhnaten's hymn.

Akhnaten marks another step on Glass's road away from minimalism and toward the mainstream. There is an almost neo-Romantic expressive force to the turbulent orchestral accompaniment and the soaring vocal lyricism – a Romanticism that sometimes grates awkwardly against the repetitive minimalist arpeggios that churn away beneath. Still, this sort of darkly brooding emotionalism would characterize many of Glass's works of the 1980s, and it was well suited to the increasingly traditional operatic and symphonic world in which he worked.

Akhnaten's birth in Stuttgart in 1984 was as resplendent as the sun-God Aten himself, but its second production – a joint venture of the Houston Grand Opera, the New York City Opera and the English National Opera – nearly buried Akhnaten's ruins once and for all. Directed by the young Australian David Freeman, the second

Akhnaten put the Pharaoh in a hermaphroditic body-suit at once hideous and absurd; it also sought to convey the timelessness of Egyptian culture by having brick-making and wheat-threshing constantly enacted onstage. The critic Tim Page wrote that this *Akhnaten* 'resembled a Saturday Night Live sketch – "The Coneheads Go to Egypt" – and featured such innovations as real puddles onstage (which were splashed every few seconds so the audience didn't forget they were there) and a pile of straw in the corner of the stage which a man would occasionally walk to and throw into the air.' Not until the CBS recording of *Akhnaten* was released in 1987 did the opera begin to be rehabilitated, although even today it still, to some degree, lingers in *Satyagraha*'s shadow.

With his trilogy complete, Philip Glass was now the best-known and most sought-after living composer. Official certification of his new celebrity status arrived in 1982, when Glass became only the third composer in history (his predecessors were Igor Stravinsky and Aaron Copland) to sign an exclusive recording contract with CBS Masterworks. Glass's plan was to lure CBS into recording his big, multi-disk operatic projects by alternating them with smaller, more commercial enterprises. His debut on the label was the lightweight instrumental album *Glassworks*, designed to introduce his music to a broader public.

Eadweard Muybridge's Victorian motion studies were the inspiration for Glass's music-theatre work *The Photographer* (1982).

So successful was *Glassworks* – by 1986, it had sold more than 175,000 copies – that CBS agreed to invest the money required to record *Satyagraha* and *Akhnaten*. (Although the Glass/CBS marriage began with much fanfare, it turned sour after CBS was bought by Sony and the new parent company appeared to lose interest in its resident composer. Glass signed with Nonesuch in 1993, creating an unusual situation in which four competing minimalists – Glass, Reich, John Adams and Louis Andriessen – all have contracts with the same label.)

By the time of the première of *Akhnaten* in 1984, Glass was producing new works in many different media at an extraordinarily rapid pace. Consider, for example, the number of projects that were on his plate in the early 1980s. His music-theatre works included *The Photographer* (1982), an odd hybrid of play, slide-show and dance inspired by the pioneering motion-studies of Victorian photographer Eadweard Muybridge; the Rome section of Robert Wilson's twelve-hour internationally-produced epic *the CIVIL warS* (1983); and *The Juniper Tree* (1984), an adaptation of a particularly grisly Brothers Grimm fairy tale composed in collaboration with Robert Moran. His dance works included *Dance* (1979), a three-way collaboration among Glass, choreographer Lucinda Childs and minimalist artist Sol LeWitt; *Glass Pieces* (1983), a ballet designed by Jerome Robbins from existing music; *A Descent into the Maelstrom* (1985), a dance-theatre realization of Poe's story for choreographer Molissa Fenley; and *In the Upper Room* (1986), for Twlya Tharp. He made his first forays into the realm of film, writing the scores for Godfrey Reggio's ecological epic *Koyanisqaatsi* (1981) and Paul Schrader's *Mishima* (1984). But with *The Olympian* he may have reached more listeners in three minutes than with all these other projects combined: commissioned by the Olympic Committee, it was played at the opening and closing ceremonies of the 1984 Summer Olympics in Los Angeles.

Of all these scores, perhaps the finest is *Koyaanisqatsi*, for it allowed Glass to transpose his penchant for non-narrative drama into a cinematic context. Directed by Godfrey Reggio, an ex-priest who became a social worker and street activist, *Koyaanisqatsi* takes its title from the Hopi Indian language, and it translates approximately as 'life out of balance'. The film, which has no dialogue or plot, contrasts placid, panoramic photography of unspoiled nature at its grandest with hyperkinetic scenes of urban life and environmental despoilation

A hyper-kinetic scene
of urban life from
Godfrey Reggio's film
Koyaanisqatsi (1981),
for which Philip Glass
wrote one of his most
successful scores

– and lets the images speak for themselves. What sounds like a simple-minded notion turned out to be suprisingly compelling, thanks in no small part to Glass's score. Reggio gave Glass unprecedented power in shaping *Koyaanisqatsi*, even going so far as to cut some scenes to fit his music. And the score itself, written for a solo bass (who intones the title word), chorus, and orchestra, is dark, sombre and unabashedly Romantic in its expressive power, capturing both the calm of nature and the ferocity of technology run amok. (Glass's two subsequent collaborations with Reggio would prove less successful: *Powaqqatsi* [1987], a simplistic comparison of idealized third-world agrarian societies with dehumanized Western urban ones, accompanied by a score overburdened with exotic instruments of every variety; and *Anima Mundi* [1991], a short film about the diversity of animal life.)

By the mid-1980s, Glass's personal life had begun to stabilize, and it is entirely possible that the intensity with which he composed was due in some measure to his new-found happiness. His marriage to Joanne Akalaitis had yielded two children, Juliet and Zachary, but had crumbled during the 1970s. In 1980 Glass married Luba Burtyk, a physician, but that relationship also proved ill-fated. It was not until 1982 that he met the artist Candy Jernigan, seemingly the woman of his dreams, although they decided to cohabit rather than marry. In 1984 Glass purchased a nineteenth-century townhouse in Manhattan's East Village, and he, Juliet, Zachary and Jernigan settled down to create a home. (Their experiment would be tragically short-lived: Jernigan died of cancer in 1991 at the age of thirty-nine, only a few months after she and Glass finally were married.)

Even today the East Village remains trendy but seedy, a low-rent district favoured by artists, intellectuals and bohemians. But it can also be a forbidding neighbourhood plagued by urban blight and social unrest, and Glass's house is located on a particularly grim corner, close to the city-run men's shelter and the Hell's Angels headquarters. Still, his small, fenced-in backyard offers some solace from the hysteria of nearby Second Avenue, and Glass, when interviewed at home, is at his most relaxed. Amiable, informal and disarmingly sincere, he greets a stranger warmly and immediately puts him at ease. Like Reich he communicates at top speed, formulating his thoughts in lengthy but impressively articulate sentences. There is nothing of the tortured or driven artist about this down-to-earth man, someone whose strictly disciplined creative life would seem to have reduced composition to a science.

When Glass is not on the road with his Ensemble, he divides his time between New York and his home on Nova Scotia's Cape Breton Island. And he further subdivides his workday with methodical precision. 'I work best in the early morning, so I compose from when I get up until noon or so, then deal with music business matters in the afternoon.' Glass composes so rapidly that he tends to overextend himself, and his veritable hyperactivity may explain the fact that, in his lesser works, he falls back on recycling existing formulas rather than creating something genuinely new. 'Occasionally I will have to write really quickly,' he admitted in 1988. 'I once wrote and recorded forty-five minutes' worth of incidental music in a week. The guys in the studio were working three hours behind me. I'd finish a move-ment, and they'd learn it and record it. I do compose quickly, you know, but nobody likes to work that fast.'

Glass's most overtly commercial endeavour, however, did not reach fruition quickly. *Songs from Liquid Days* took from February to December 1985 to complete, far longer than Glass had anticipated when he agreed to the project. For it was not his idea. The notion of Glass composing a collection of pop songs was proposed by CBS, partly as a way of paying for the recording of *Satyagraha*. Glass, in turn, was smart enough to realize that pop songs depended on pop lyricists, and so he approached Paul Simon, Suzanne Vega, Laurie Anderson and David Byrne as collaborators. Once the songs were completed, Glass spent months searching for the right singer for each number, eventually settling on Linda Ronstadt, The Roches, Janice Pendarvis (who worked with Sting), Bernard Fowler (of Herbie Hancock's group), and his one-time Gandhi, Douglas Perry. This motley assortment of singers is at the mercy of lyrics that, in most cases, seem arty and pretentious, as if the writers were intimidated by the idea of working with a highbrow composer.

Still, no one could accuse Glass of selling out to CBS's commercial ambitions. 'Everybody was hoping that somehow, accidentally, I would write a hit song,' he said. 'It really doesn't work that way … You get a guy like me who's spent his life working in the theatre, and he's not going to suddenly write a hit. The most common reaction to the record is "Boy, is that unusual."' The six songs last up to ten minutes, far longer than radio play-lists allow, and are accompanied not by electric guitars or drums but by an enlarged Philip Glass Ensemble that occasionally includes the Kronos Quartet. The result is more of a classically-conceived song-cycle than a pop-oriented concept album.

But in composing *Songs from Liquid Days*, Glass had an ulterior motive: to gain experience in setting the English language. After years of dealing with arcane tongues, he was now about to embark on his first full-length opera in English, *The Making of the Representative for Planet 8* (1986). Moreover, the writer Doris Lessing (whose *Planet 8* is the fourth instalment in her series of science-fiction allegories, *Canopus in Argos*) provided Glass with an extraordinarily dense libretto. Even after spending a year streamlining that libretto, which went through six drafts and an expansion from two to three acts, Glass knew that he would have an awful lot of English to set.

Like his previous music-theatre works, *Planet 8* is less a narrative drama than an opera of spiritual ideas. 'The plot is simple', Glass said. 'It's the story of a planet that is entering an ice age through what Lessing calls a "cosmological disaster." It's basically about a race of people who are about to die, about a planet that is losing the heat of the sun … People face their death, the death of their species. But there are many different ways of dying.' Indeed, a select few of the citizens of Planet 8 are chosen to become Representatives – free-floating entities who will survive the death of their planet and become quasi-Jungian repositories for its collective wisdom.

Clearly, *Planet 8* is more an allegory about life on earth than a tale about extra-terrestrials. But it hardly seemed promising as an opera. Static and anti-dramatic, it concerns itself not so much with visceral events as with ponderous philosophical musings. And Glass's setting of English proved to be stiff and awkward, its sing-song prosody making the wordiness of the libretto more apparent. Perhaps it is an indication of Glass's desperation that he set huge chunks of the libretto as spoken dialogue above orchestral accompaniment.

When *Planet 8* finally received its première in July 1988, it was not a critical success. But by this point no criticism could slow the frenetic pace of Glass's career. In May 1988 Glass's one-act chamber-opera *The Fall of the House of Usher*, based on Poe's short story, was given its first performances; and in July 1988 Glass's one-act melodrama, *1000*

Airplanes on the Roof, was presented at Hangar No. 3 of the Schwechat International Airport in Vienna. Cast for a speaking actor and a small, amplified ensemble, *1000 Airplanes* marked Glass's debut as a director. He gave designer Jerome Sirlin (best known for his direction of Madonna's 1987 'Who's That Girl?' tour) the task of turning an airplane hangar into an ominous, hallucinatory cityscape, and Sirlin, inspired by the work's sci-fi subject, used holographic projections in place of conventional sets.

Perhaps still smarting from the criticism aimed at *Planet 8,* Glass admitted that setting English remained difficult for him. And *1000 Airplanes* was more of an evasion of the problem than a solution. 'I'm trying to invent a way for English to be used as a viable music-theater language,' he said, seeming to imply that no previous composer had ever set English successfully. '*Usher* was sung, *The Representative* used a mixture of speech and song, and *1000 Airplanes* is spoken. But I'm still finding my way.'

In March 1988, New York's Metropolitan Opera – an institution so conservative that it had presented only two new operas in twenty-six seasons – announced that it had commissioned Glass to write an opera commemorating the 500th anniversary of Columbus's discovery of America. The Met's surprising decision vindicated the confident prediction with which Glass ended his 1987 book, *Music by Philip Glass.* 'I don't doubt that the world of traditional opera will eventually be dragged – probably screaming – into the twentieth century,' he had written. 'Of course, by then it will be the twenty-first century.' As it turned out, it did not take quite that long.

Scheduled for a première on the quincentenary itself – 12 October 1992, known in America as Columbus Day – *The Voyage* would mark Glass's first return to the Met since *Einstein on the Beach* was presented in 1976. Then, however, Glass had crept in through the back door, since the Met had been rented for the occasion. Now the Met had flung its front door wide open, and was giving him $325,000 for *The Voyage,* reputedly the most money ever paid for a new opera. Even Verdi, who received (in 1992 dollars) the equivalent of $225,000 for *Aida,* would have to take second place.

Glass, as usual overburdened with new projects, could not turn to *The Voyage* until he had completed a number of outstanding commitments. There was a film score for Errol Morris, *The Thin Blue Line*

(1988), depicting the true story of a man's wrongful conviction for the murder of a Dallas policeman. There were two vividly programmatic orchestral works, *The Canyon* (1988) and *Itaipu* (1989), the latter a forty-minute 'symphonic portrait for chorus and orchestra' inspired by a massive new dam on the border of Brazil and Paraguay. And, most importantly, there was a collaboration with the archetypal American beat poet, Allen Ginsberg – titled *Hydrogen Jukebox* after a line from Ginsberg's *Howl*, 'listening to the crack of doom on the hydrogen jukebox.'

Ginsberg and Glass, both practising Tibetan Buddhists, both enamoured of India, and both liberals outraged by the 'do-nothing conservatism' of the Reagan years, made a natural pair. 'It was right after the 1988 presidential election, and neither Bush nor Dukakis seemed to talk about anything that was going on,' Glass recalled. 'I remember saying to Allen, "If these guys aren't going to talk about the issues then we should."' Eventually, Glass and Ginsberg stitched together a quasi-libretto from eighteen of Ginsberg's poems. 'Together they formed a portrait of America, at least in our eyes, that covered the fifties, sixties, seventies and eighties. It also ranged in content from highly personal poems of Allen's to his reflection of social issues: the

The quintessential beat poet Allen Ginsberg, pictured in 1966; he had written his most influential poem, *Howl*, ten years earlier.

anti-war movement, the sexual revolution, drugs, Eastern philosophy, environmental awareness.' Jerome Sirlin, fresh from *1000 Airplanes*, was engaged to provide a visual environment consisting of slide and film projections.

Perhaps it was Ginsberg's long-standing predilection for impassioned recitation that led Glass to turn once again to a spoken text with instrumental accompaniment. Some of the poems of *Hydrogen Jukebox* (1990) are in fact sung – there is a vocal ensemble of six singers used in various permutations from solos to sextets – but the most powerful numbers are left for Ginsberg to declaim in his typically ecstatic oratory. Neither solution seems entirely successful. When Glass sets Ginsberg's poems to music, the stiff rhythms entrap rather than enhance the rhapsodic words. When Glass accompanies Ginsberg's speaking, the music recedes to insignificance, a mere sonic backdrop for the poems.

With *Hydrogen Jukebox* behind him, Glass could turn in earnest to *The Voyage*. Glass's librettist was David Henry Hwang, his collaborator on *1000 Airplanes* and the author of the hit Broadway play, *M. Butterfly*. Instead of the eighty-page libretto that weighed down *Planet 8*, the text of *The Voyage* amounted to some fifteen pages – and that for three hours of music. 'I've learned a lot about librettos,' Glass said, laughing mischievously at the memory of *Planet 8*.

> *My feeling now is that I'm something of a 'minimalist' when it comes to librettos. What makes opera so wonderful is that what we're conveying isn't done only through words. The visual material, the musical setting, the dramatic staging, all those things are part of what puts the story over. In a house the size of the Met, to get into the dialectics of discovery would have been a big mistake. I wanted a piece that could tell a story in broad strokes, and had a powerful emotional punch to it.*

Glass had no desire to recount the tale of Columbus. Instead, he viewed Columbus as symbolic of a larger theme – that of the irresistible human urge toward exploration. 'I didn't want to do a historical Columbus,' Glass said. 'It seemed to me that if you wanted to know about Columbus you could go to the library. Generally speaking, the opera house isn't a particularly good place to deal with reality. What we *can* do in opera is to make it the workshop where allegory and fiction and poetry are brought to a level of the investigation of the human condition.'

After a Prologue in which a scientist muses on mankind's endless search for knowledge, *The Voyage* transports us back to the Ice Age, when a spaceship of explorers crashes on Earth – and, it is implied, leads the natives toward a higher evolution. Act Two shows Columbus at sea, consumed with doubt, interacting with a mystical Isabella. And Act Three takes us to the year 2092, when the earthlings, now possessing proof of those Ice-Age visitors, set off to the stars in search of the source of knowledge. Only in the Epilogue does Columbus, on his deathbed, reappear to consider the meaning of discovery. At the end, his bed rises up toward the stars.

There is no doubt that Glass tailored *The Voyage* to the Met's unparalleled resources – its large orchestra and eighty-voice chorus, its sophisticated technical facilities, and the sheer size of its 3800-seat hall. 'There was a strategy involved,' he admitted with the cunning of an experienced opera composer. 'The end of Act One is the biggest moment musically and dramatically in the opera. I wanted to remove any doubt in anybody's mind about the scale of this opera.'

Aside from its grandiose scale, there are other ways in which *The Voyage* explores territory new to Glass. Immediately in the Prologue, the opera establishes a dark, brooding tone, partly a reflection of its increasingly chromatic (and dissonant) harmonic palette. As a wordless female chorus soars high above, rapid scales rumble in the lower strings, building to an expanse of Sibelian starkness and sweep. Although Glass's raw material still consists of brief melodic patterns that enlarge or shrink during the course of repetition, those patterns have receded to the background – providing an accompaniment for a newly arching lyricism.

And *The Voyage*, unlike *Satyagraha*, is an opera that drives toward potent climaxes. Although the action of *The Voyage* is often more psychological than physical, its libretto is of a reasonably linear, narrative variety, and its three acts are designed so that each culminates in a moment of pageantry: the confrontation of the spaceship Commander and the Ice-Age earthlings that ends Act One, Columbus's sighting of land at the close of Act Two, and the parade of dignitaries that bids farewell to the spaceship in Act Three.

But what is more unexpected is *The Voyage*'s expressive impact. Columbus and Isabella, for instance, interact with a sensuous passion that is unprecedented in Glass's output. Even Hwang noticed the change in tone. 'I feel that there's an emotionality to *The Voyage* which I wouldn't say is lacking in Philip's work – a lot of *Satyagraha* is extremely emotional – but I think Philip has taken his signature techniques and advanced them so that they serve the purpose of a linear text more precisely,' said Hwang. 'In other words, they seem to have a momentum and a drive to them, as if they're progressing to a certain point, in the same way you expect a text of different characters to come together and reach some sort of apotheosis.'

Whether Glass sets English or Sanskrit, he favours a plain, unadorned vocal declamation that shuns all hints of virtuosity. 'There's no virtuoso singing of a traditional kind,' he said. 'I'm not even tempted to write it. To me, that draws attention away from something more essential. Opera is about voice and singing, but I don't think technical virtuosity is the most interesting thing.'

So it is no surprise that the vocal lines are seldom the focus of attention. In *The Voyage*, as in so much of Wagner, the continuous orchestral fabric retains primacy; the vocal parts themselves can seem almost incidental to the complexities unfolding around them. 'The vocal language grows out of the musical surroundings,' said Glass. Then he made an astonishing admission. 'In many cases the orchestral treatment is written first. From that I can find many vocal responses to the musical setting that the voice finds itself in.'

When Glass sets wordless vocalise – such as the Commander's ecstatic solo at the end of Act One – his vocal lines really soar. But when he is tied down to English, his prosody again seems rhythmically four-square and unidiomatic. Glass, after all, didn't set a full-length English text until *Planet 8*, and he conceded that he is still finding his way. 'English is a hard language to master, and I don't think I got it right the first time. But I think I've gotten better at it. Setting English in a colloquial way is something I'm very concerned with.'

When *The Voyage* received its eagerly anticipated world première, it was heard not only by the sold-out houses at the Met, but by a worldwide radio audience. The $2 million production was a scenic spectacular, although all too often it threatened to turn into an unintentional parody of Robert Wilson's inscrutable visual effects. But *The Voyage* was clearly Glass's most significant opera since *Akhnaten*. And it proved that Glass could still rise to his old level – if he allowed himself the time to focus his energy on a single project.

The theme of discovery remained on Glass's mind long after the *The Voyage* had been composed. Even before *The Voyage*'s première, Glass had gone on to write his tenth opera, *White Raven*, a collaboration with his *Einstein* co-creator, Robert Wilson. Commissioned by the Portuguese Government and set to a text in Portuguese (a language that Glass speaks), the five-act *White Raven* again deals with exploration, although in a typically enigmatic, Wilsonian manner. This time the main character is the fifteenth-century Portuguese explorer Vasco da Gama, who sailed around Africa and established a maritime route to India. But Wilson, never one to engage in a conventional linear narrative, introduces a cast of characters that includes Miss Universe, the Tinman, a dragon, and Judy Garland. 'It's more like a series of visual and aural fantasies about travelling to different parts of the world,' Glass said with a bemused smile.

Beauty (Josette Day) and the Beast (Jean Marais) in Jean Cocteau's film *La Belle et la Bête* (1946), which Philip Glass transformed into an opera in 1993

Jean Cocteau – film-maker, writer, artist and misunderstood genius – in 1956

It was perhaps a desire to make a more profound, internal journey toward self-discovery that led Glass to undertake his next project – a trilogy of music-theatre pieces based on the films of Jean Cocteau. Glass took the original screenplays of Cocteau's three greatest films – *Orphée* (1949), *La Belle et la Bête* (1946), and *Les Enfants terribles* (1950) – and made from them, in turn, a chamber opera, a film with music, and a ballet. Why would Glass turn to Cocteau? Perhaps because he identified with the great French artist – a man who was resented not only for his success in many different media but for his sheer fluency, a man who saw himself as a misunderstood genius.

Glass described his trilogy as a 'homage to Cocteau, whom I think of as an important twentieth-century artist. In his time he was thought of as being too facile: he wrote poetry and plays and novels, he painted, and he directed movies. And people quite incorrectly thought he was a dilettante. Today the French are dismissive and protective of him at the same time. But remember, even by 1954 when I went to Paris for the first time, Cocteau was already considered passé. The film *Orphée* is an autobiographical work about an older artist displaced by a younger one. And whom is he killed by at the end? His fellow poets. When Orphée asserts to the critic that he's adored by the public, the critic says "But the public is alone." (A wonderful line).' The parallel is irresistible: Glass, after all, has similarly been vilified by both composers and critics – yet loved by his audience.

Cocteau's screenplay for *Orphée* is preserved, almost word for word, as the libretto for Glass's opera, a small-scale work scored for twelve instrumentalists and four soloists. Not since *Satyagraha* has Glass created a score of such jewel-like perfection, and one has to wonder if the reason lies in the confluence of the personal and the professional. Certainly Glass identifies with Cocteau, but he must also identify with Orpheus himself, the musician who tries to lead his dead wife from the Underworld back to the land of the living. Glass's own wife, Candy Jernigan, died the year before he composed *Orphée*, and one can only suspect that Orpheus's grief must have resembled the composer's own. Whatever the reason, *Orphée* (1992) displays a transparency of texture, a subtlety of instrumental colour, and, most importantly, a newly expressive and unfettered vocal writing. There is an understated dignity and reserve to Glass's conception, as if he had been inspired as much by Gluck's opera *Orfeo ed Euridice* (1762) as by Cocteau.

The next instalment in the trilogy, *La Belle et la Bête* (1993), is less subtle but more high-tech. This time Glass took Cocteau's classic film, stripped it of both its dialogue and Georges Auric's original music, and wrote a new score of his own. In Glass's version, the vocalists and instrumentalists stand in front of a backstage projection of Cocteau's film, and sing the screenplay while the characters onscreen merely mouth it. Although this combination of live music and film presents problems of synchronization (and can lead to some unintentionally amusing results), it suggests a hybrid art-form with many possibilities for the future. 'There have been silent movies with live music before but, as far as I know, no one has actually opera-ized a movie,' said Glass.

La Belle et la Bête marks Glass's twelfth opera; when he completes one more, he will have equalled Wagner's output. Lately, however, he has shown a new (and rather belated) interest in orchestral music, and his operatic production has slowed accordingly. Not until 1987 did Glass begin composing orchestral scores – *The Light*, a symphonic poem commissioned by the Cleveland Orchestra; and a Violin Concerto for Paul Zukofsky. *The Canyon* (1988), a *Concerto Grosso* (1992), the *'Low' Symphony* (1992) and the Symphony No. 2 (1994) all followed in quick succession. But Glass, never less than prolific, cautioned: 'This is really the beginning of my symphonic output.'

Glass performing in London
in 1992

By far the most successful of these works is the *Low' Symphony*, which has a compositional genesis that must be nearly unique in the annals of classical music. Glass took three instrumental numbers from the pathbreaking David Bowie/Brian Eno album *Low* (1977), and used them to provide the thematic material for his symphony. Bowie and Eno first heard Glass during his visit to London in 1971, and *Low* was profoundly influenced by Glass's brand of minimalism. Now, nearly two decades later, Glass returned the favour. The borrowed themes are subjected to Glass's own brand of repetition and transformation, but what makes the work so successful is that Glass develops his material in a genuinely symphonic fashion, gradually building toward impassioned climaxes and extended thematic statements. The mood is prevailingly melancholy and wistful, and the arching lyricism evokes some unlikely comparisons – a post-Romantic English symphonist like Ralph Vaughan Williams, or an American symphonist like Aaron Copland.

If only the Symphony No. 2 had been as successful. But it brought to the surface, yet again, the predicament of Glass's recent style. In the

1970s, when his whirling, raucous minimalist patterns were put to the
service of lean, mean repetition, they seemed shockingly audacious,
a smack in the face to the pretentions of the entire classical-music
world. In the 1980s, when those patterns became the stuff of opera,
they worked best when they were not inflated to bombastic proportions: that is why *Satyagraha* is more successful than *The Voyage*. But
the operas, after all, have vocal lines that tend to push the repetitive
patterns into an accompanimental function. In Glass's orchestral
works, the descending scales, burbling arpeggios, and predictable
syncopations are not background to anything – and when they are
dressed up in grandiose orchestral garb, there is an all-too-apparent
disparity between the deliberately simple material and the climactic,
frankly Romantic expressive aspirations.

The three-movement, forty-minute Symphony No. 2 is remarkably conventional and even banal, a virtual embrace of the conservative European tradition that Glass once shunned. Clearly Glass is no
longer writing for an audience that seeks the new or provocative.

Instead he is aiming for a mainstream that, to his credit, is of his own
making – a large and devoted public that expects a familiar style and
is not disappointed when it gets it. It is an enviable position for a
living composer to find himself in, but not one that encourages risk-
taking. Neither *Music in Twelve Parts* nor *Einstein* could have arisen
in an environment as stultifyingly predictable as this one.

So what is one to make of Philip Glass? The critic John Rockwell
framed the problem best when he wrote in 1993 that 'the question
is whether Mr. Glass has simply declined, or has declined in an interesting way, or has sold out, or is just uneven, or is groping toward
a promising new idiom.' Rockwell did not answer his own question,
but he did conclude that Glass's 'faith in the compelling power of
expansive repetition has been subverted by a desire to appeal to a
mainstream audience.'

Steve Reich roused himself from his conventional orchestral works
of the 1980s, and in the 1990s recaptured the spirit of innovation that
had marked his early compositions; certainly there was nothing
predictable nor comfortable about *Different Trains* or *The Cave*. But
Glass now seems less interested in innovation. Not since the early
1980s has he composed something that could be said to be shockingly
new and unexpected, and his reward has been a public of unsurpassed

size and enthusiasm. The price has been a bland sameness of style – a far cry from the cutting edge he occupied in the 1970s.

Perhaps that has been his intention all along. His own comments, in fact, may go further toward explaining his present status than any convoluted critical analysis. 'I started out being an experimental composer, but now I'm very much a populist composer,' he said in 1987. And in 1988, he clearly indicated his direction for the 1990s: 'I reserve the right to change my work through my career. Every artist does. There may have been a misconception all along. I never intended to remain a "subtle" artist. My intention was always to look for a broader public. Basically, that's what I've done.'

6

The post-minimalist
composer John Adams at
the keyboard

*Minimalism was a wonderful shock to Western
art music. It was like a bucket of fresh spring
water splashed on the grim and rigid visage of
serious music. I can't imagine how stark and
unforgiving the musical landscape would be like
without it. But I think that as an expressive tool
the style absolutely had to evolve and become
more complex.*

John Adams, in a 1992 interview

Adams, Monk and Post-Minimalism

One of John Adams's earliest memories is of sitting in the living room of his rural New England home and listening to recordings. 'I was about three when LPs were invented,' he recalled. 'I clearly remember my father coming home with a turntable and two albums. One was Leopold Stokowski doing the *1812 Overture*, and the other was Bozo the Clown conducting John Philip Sousa circus marches. Before long I was conducting the phonograph with my mother's knitting needle.' Adams interrupted this recollection to add a pointed and revealing observation: 'I grew up in a household where Benny Goodman and Mozart were not separated.'

It is precisely that openness to every variety of music – American and European, old and new, 'high' art and 'low' pop – that makes John Adams's compositions so different from those of his minimalist predecessors. The term *post-minimalism* has been invented to describe Adams's eclectic vocabulary, one in which the austerity of minimalism now rubs shoulders with the passion of Romanticism. Turn-of-the-century post-Romantics like Mahler and Sibelius took nineteenth-century Romanticism but altered it by embracing elements of early twentieth-century style. And John Adams, a generation younger than Reich and Glass, has similarly inherited the minimalist vocabulary and enriched it with a new expressive power and an impudent delight in stylistic juxtapositions. 'To be a modern composer you have to be able to move with promiscuous ease through all these different musical experiences,' Adams said. 'And you have to be able to laugh at yourself.'

Music critics have rarely been known to laugh, which may explain why Adams has often found himself pilloried by the journalistic establishment. His crime, it would seem, lies in having taken the impersonal, rigorous and stylistically pure language of early minimalism and rendered it impure – a steaming compost heap of late twentieth-century American musical culture. The American critic Edward Rothstein described this process as 'the trashing of minimalism', and it is true that in Adams's music minimalism becomes only one style among many.

To understand Adams's irreverent eclecticism, one has to take
a longer view that extends back to his childhood. Born in Worcester,
Massachusetts on 15 February 1947, Adams had musical parents.

*My father was a jazz sax player. In fact, that's how he met my mother.
My grandfather, her stepfather, owned a dance hall in New Hampshire up
on Lake Winnipesaukee. It was called* Irwin's Winnipesaukee Gardens,
*and it had a gorgeous hardwood dance floor built out on pilings over the
lake. It was incredibly romantic. All the big bands came up during the
30s and 40s and played there all summer long. My father came up
playing clarinet and saxophone in a B band – the backup band for a big
band. And my mother was there, singing with another band. They met
and eloped. So my first musical experiences as a very small child were a
combination of classical music, which both of my parents loved, and jazz.*

John Adams in a
characteristically impudent
mood

When Adams was still a child, his family moved from Worcester, near Boston, to Woodstock, Vermont and, finally, to the rural isolation of East Concord, New Hampshire. An archetypal New England village with a town common, white-steepled churches, and 300 people, East Concord would be Adams's home until he went to college.

Considering the size of East Concord, Adams was offered an extraordinary array of musical opportunities. First came the clarinet, which his father began teaching him when he was eight years old. By the age of eleven he had written his first composition, and he would wander through the snow-covered pine forests outside his house, imagining the opus numbers of yet-to-be-composed symphonies. Soon Adams joined his father in Concord's marching band, and in his early teens he was promoted to the position of first clarinet.

By the time Adams was a teenager, his skills as a clarinettist, composer, and conductor were put to use in a community orchestra sponsored by the New Hampshire State Mental Hospital. Adams was the only youngster in an otherwise adult orchestra, and he was given the opportunity to conduct his first large-scale composition, a three-movement Suite for String Orchestra, written when he was thirteen. 'I think the people in the orchestra and the adults in the Concord community recognized me as a prodigy, and were excited that this kid who was so young could compose and conduct as well as play the clarinet.'

The orchestra taught Adams some useful musical lessons. One concert demonstrated that music possessed a profound expressive potential. 'We'd be playing the most banal piece of music, and I'd look out and see people with tears running down their faces. My music has always been that way, and I think that's why it threatens so many people. My music is emotionally committed.'

And another concert reminded Adams of the sheer lunacy that can lurk beneath even the most polished surface. The orchestra included a few mental patients, whom Adams remembers as 'fabulous wild cards'.

We'd be playing through the Unfinished Symphony *by Schubert or selections from* Carousel *and suddenly one of the patients – especially this guy behind me, who played the clarinet – would just simply go* off. *Anything. He might start glossolalia – yadayadayadyayadya – or else play his clarinet desperately fast. Nobody ever got upset, nobody ever had to be*

The conductor and composer Leonard Bernstein, in 1966

hauled away in a straitjacket, but here are these nice polite New England folk and they're all sawing away and there's always this wonderful consciousness of what might happen around the corner: somebody's going to – AAAHHHHHHHH! That was my first experience of music as a social activity: that within something very profound and meaningful, the utterly insane can still happen.

A passion for American popular culture, a respect for the emotional power of music, and a fondness for the unexpected: the seeds of Adams's future compositional career had been planted before he finished high school. Now it was left for Harvard to try to uproot them.

Already as a teenager, Adams had been travelling to Boston to study the clarinet with Felix Viscuglia of the Boston Symphony Orchestra. Now he received a scholarship to Harvard University, the Ivy League bastion that had propelled composers like Leonard Bernstein, Walter Piston and Elliott Carter on their path to fame. Neither of Adams's parents had college degrees, and to them the prospect of their son going to a prestigious university was positively dazzling.

So off he went, intending to focus his musical energies on conducting and the clarinet. At first he continued his clarinet playing, joining the Boston Symphony as a freelancer (his most potent memory is of playing in the American première of Schoenberg's opera *Moses und Aron*), and being a soloist with the Harvard-Radcliffe Orchestra in the first performances of Piston's Clarinet Concerto. Soon conducting got the better of him, and he directed a student performance of Mozart's *Marriage of Figaro* in the dining hall of his Harvard house. At that point one of Bernstein's unofficial talent scouts noticed Adams – and the maestro invited him to come to Tanglewood, the Boston Symphony's summer home, as a conducting fellow.

Hardly anyone would decline such an invitation. But during the summer of 1967 – which Adams, by now 'a hippie in all but wearing beads', remembers as a season filled with self-examination and drug experimentation – he decided to become a composer, not a conductor. 'The first big thing I did was a setting for chamber orchestra and soprano, a song cycle based on psychedelic poems by a friend of mine at Harvard,' he recalled with a laugh. 'They all sounded like something halfway between Jim Morrison's The Doors and *Sgt. Pepper's*.' By

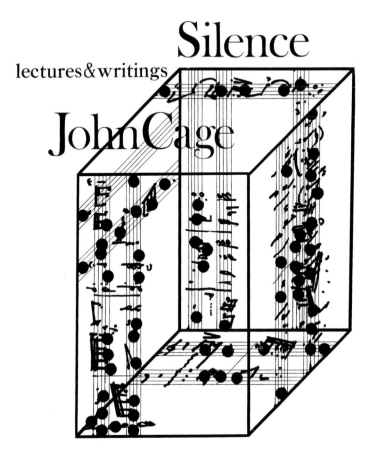

The cover of John Cage's book *Silence*, which dropped into Adams's psyche 'like a time bomb'

now Adams had immersed himself in rock, and he even interviewed Cream for *The Harvard Crimson.* 'Over fifty percent of my listening was rock. I was much inspired by certain albums that appeared to me to have a fabulous unity to them, like *Disraeli Gears, Abbey Road, Dark Side of the Moon*, and Marvin Gaye's *What's Going On?'*

Needless to say, this was not the sort of music that Harvard's music department was promoting. There the twelve-note composition of Arnold Schoenberg and his disciples still held sway. 'It was a period of profound cognitive dissonance,' Adams said with a touch of bitterness.

Because the teachers were just totally out of touch with what was going on in popular culture and American culture. I was interested in

*jazz and rock, and then I would go into the music department, which was
like a mausoleum where we would sit and count tone-rows in Webern. It
was a dreadful time. But then we were all going back to our rooms and
getting high and listening to Cecil Taylor and John Coltrane and the
Rolling Stones. It struck me as ironic that there was so much feeling in
rock – that rock expressed our Dionysian side, expressed our spiritual side,
and our convivial, social side, but in the serious contemporary music that
I was being taught, feeling had become extremely refined and so restrained
and so sublimated and so complicated. Right from 1967 I knew I was
leading a double life – and that it was dishonest.*

Adams's draft notice arrived during his last semester as an undergraduate student and, instead of going off to fight in Vietnam, he
reluctantly decided to seek shelter in Harvard's music programme.
Even though he admired his composition teacher, Leon Kirchner, he
recalls the atmosphere as akin to 'a malignant cocoon'. By the time he
received his master's degree in 1971 he was positively seething with a
desire for change.

Change came from an unlikely direction. As a graduation present,
his parents gave him John Cage's book *Silence*, which 'dropped into
my psyche like a time bomb'. Cage did not provide answers, but he
asked provocative questions about what sounds constituted music –
questions that had not been posed at Harvard. Suddenly Adams
sensed that there might be alternatives to the sterile modernism with
which he had been indoctrinated. And, like Reich a generation earlier,
he felt that in San Francisco he might find the freedom to explore
those options.

So in the summer of 1971 Adams packed up his Volkswagen Beetle
and drove cross-country to San Francisco. (Apparently, the laid-back
Northern California life-style has appealed to this introspective New
Englander, for to this day Adams has never left the Bay Area.) At first
his life there was anything but promising. For more than a year he
composed nothing, and in order to earn a living he worked in a water-
front warehouse – unpacking Bermuda shorts, which were in transit
from Taiwan to Sears.

Things looked bleak, but suddenly 'a job just dropped in my lap.'
The San Francisco Conservatory of Music, at that time a financially
pressed but artistically adventurous institution, was seeking young,

equally adventurous faculty members, and Adams fitted the bill. For ten years, from 1972 to 1982, Adams's musical life revolved around the Conservatory, where he was made head of the new-music programme. He conducted the orchestra and new-music ensemble, taught analysis and orchestration and composition, and led the 'obliging young students … on an avant-garde crusade dedicated to burning down the last bastions of stylistic authority and musical formalism.' For Adams, the Conservatory became one gigantic compositional laboratory in which he could experiment with impunity – and, eventually, find his own voice.

At first he turned to a Cage-inspired investigation of unconventional sound sources, just as Young had done more than a decade before. *American Standard* (1973), named after a brand of toilet and scored for an anarchic and unspecified ensemble, took American 'standards' – a march, a hymn, a ballad – and stripped them of their familiar ingredients. More radical, and reeking of Adams's typical insouciance, was *Lo-Fi* (1975). 'The idea was to create music out of found sonic objects, so we went to Goodwill stores and bought old 78-rpm discs of Frank Sinatra and trashed-up record players and broken speakers that had been yanked out of car dashboards, and we made this enormous sonic environment in a big auditorium in Golden Gate Park.' After the performance, Adams received some unexpected advice: 'An incoming student for the following year offered to give me composition lessons!'

Next Adams turned to electronic instruments, going so far as to design integrated circuitry and build his own synthesizer. After a three-year immersion in electronics, he experienced what he calls a 'diatonic conversion' – an emphatic realization of the power of tonality, which he now views as a veritable force of nature. 'Electronics made me realize the resonant power of consonance … We all learned in college that tonality died, somewhere around the same time that Nietzsche's God died. And I believed it. When you make a dogmatic decision like that early in your life, it takes some kind of powerful experience to undo it, and mine was working with the synthesizer.'

But after five years of crafting Cageian chaos and electronic collages, Adams found himself at a dead end. How would he put to use his renewed faith in tonality? What musical language might be available to him? Fortunately there was one new style that was tonal, consonant, pulsating with the rhythms of American popular culture, and cutting-edge. It was called minimalism. Adams had just begun to get familiar with it – and it changed his life for good.

Back at Harvard, Adams had already heard the recording of Riley's *In C.* But it was not until Steve Reich and Musicians came to San Francisco in 1974 to perform *Drumming* that Adams became a convert. The next year he heard a concert by the Philip Glass Ensemble, and he began to wonder if minimalism might offer a solution to his creative dilemma. 'I can't begin to describe how stuck I was before that, doing big, messy tape collages and fooling around with chance principles – having fun, but feeling somehow that I hadn't found the deepest level of myself. It was exciting to think that maybe there was a way out of that pretty grim period.'

What impressed Adams most about Reich's *Drumming* and *Music for Mallet Instruments, Voices and Organ* (which he conducted in 1977) was the highly accessible combination of clear tonality and steady pulsation on the one hand, and bracing structural rigour on the other. Even today he speaks of minimalism as 'the only really interesting important stylistic development in the past thirty years. As much as people would like to deny it, it is responsible for a revolution in music.'

Almost immediately, however, it became clear that Adams would take that revolution in a direction very different from either Reich or Glass. Less involved with non-Western music, Adams immediately turned minimalist techniques to the service of much more emotional, climactic, and directionalized musical language. He rejected the mechanistic impersonality of early minimalist pieces, which had been built around musical procedures so pure that, in Reich's words, 'once the process is set up and loaded, it runs by itself.' Instead, Adams's restless personality broke the bonds of musical process, demanded a more rapid degree of change, and revelled in an 'impure' range of stylistic possibilities. 'I'm trying to embrace the tragic aspects of life in my work,' he said in 1985. 'That's something that minimalism has not really succeeded in doing yet.'

All these elements are apparent in Adams's first two minimalist essays, the piano piece *Phrygian Gates* (1977–8), and the string septet *Shaker Loops* (1978). Both nearly a half-hour long, they showed what Adams intended to do with his inherited minimalist vocabulary.

Two of the last surviving residents of a New Hampshire community of Shakers; the ecstatic rituals of this sect inspired Adams's *Shaker Loops* (1978).

Phrygian Gates roamed through a cycle of seven different keys, and in each one Adams highlighted the emotional disparity between two of the ancient Greek modes, the Lydian ('light, sensual, resonant') and the Phrygian ('volatile, unstable, but often more heroic'). Although *Phrygian Gates* unfolded as a nearly unbroken chain of pulsating eighth notes, its harmonic variety and its impassioned climaxes left minimalism behind.

Shaker Loops went even farther in charting Adams's independent course. The title refers to the Shakers, an eighteenth-century New England fundamentalist sect whose ecstatic rituals induced quivering and trembling; 'loops' alludes to the notation of the score, written as a series of repeated modules, each resembling a miniature tape loop. But instead of turning this structure into a highly rational, slowly unfolding Reichian process, Adams kept his modules in a state of flux, shifting unexpectedly from bustling rhythms to motionless pools of sound. In the third movement, when the cellos burst forth with melodies of radiant, long-limbed lyricism, Adams made clear that his brand of minimalism would embrace the full range of expressive possibilities available to a late-twentieth-century composer.

To Adams, the minimalism of Reich and Glass offered immense opportunities for growth – and he, a generation younger than the pioneers, might be able to develop the language in a way that they had not. 'I think minimalism was a wonderful shock to Western art music,' he said in 1992.

It was like a bucket of fresh spring water splashed on the grim and rigid visage of serious music. I can't imagine how stark and unforgiving the musical landscape would be like without it. But I think that as an expressive tool the style absolutely had to evolve and become more complex. This is inevitable in art. Monteverdi, Mozart, Hemingway, Le Corbusier ... they all brought about revolutions in simplicity, une révolution en douceur, *but then they were immediately followed by a second, more complex generation.*

What has caused such controversy is not the fact that Adams sees himself as the man who will bring greater intricacy to the elegant simplicity of minimalism. It is how he goes about introducing that complexity. Adams, who grew up inundated with recordings of every variety, views all music – austere minimalism and poignant post-Romanticism, the nostalgic strains of big-band swing and the motoric pulsation of rock – as being grist for his creative mill. Rather than filtering those influences through strict minimalist processes, he embraces them whole-heartedly. The result is an unpredictable music filled with emotive outbursts and stylistic disparities. And to those who uphold the ascetic, self-abnegating purity of minimalism, Adams seems no better than a traitor to the cause.

Adams freely acknowledges his debt to Reich and Glass, and he remains on friendly terms with both. But he feels that he had to reach beyond them.

What sets me apart from Reich and Glass is that I am not a modernist. I embrace the whole musical past, and I don't have the kind of refined, systematic language that they have. I rely a lot more on my intuitive sense of balance. I've stopped worrying about whether intuiting a structure is right or not; as far as I can tell, most nineteenth-century composers wrote on intuitive levels.

From Adams's perspective, composers like Reich and Glass began their careers as archetypal modernists. Just like their enemies the twelve-note serialists, they were seeking a systematic method for con-

A portrait of John Adams
taken in his studio at home
in Berkeley, California

structing music, and their watchword was originality – the rallying cry of the avant garde. But for Adams this grail-like quest for originality is no longer an issue. 'All of my music has this feeling of *déjà vu*. The issue of vanguardism, the whole avant garde, has burned itself out. As we approach the end of this century, there is an exhaustion of this intense need to run to the barricades, to forge ahead to the future.' Instead, Adams sees his position as analogous to Mahler, Bach, and Brahms, who 'were standing at the end of an era and were embracing all of the evolutions that occurred over the previous thirty to fifty years.'

In 1978 Adams became new-music adviser to the San Francisco Symphony and its conductor, Edo de Waart; from 1982 to 1985, his position was formalized as composer-in-residence. During those years, the Symphony commissioned from Adams two orchestral scores. The first, *Harmonium* (1981), ended up being a three-movement work for huge chorus and orchestra that required some 275 performers. And the second, *Harmonielehre* (1985), was a three-movement orchestral piece that sprawled over nearly forty minutes.

Both display an unlikely synthesis of minimalism and post-Romanticism – a merger so personal that it can be recognized as Adams's own after hearing only a few bars of music. *Harmonium*, set to texts by John Donne and Emily Dickinson, is filled with thunder-ous climaxes whose manic intensity can be positively terrifying. Here the pulsating rhythms and the repetitive minimalist patterns recede to the background, and the expansive lyricism that grabs the foreground reveals the subjective side of Adams's personality for the first time.

Harmonielehre, however, is even more surprising. Named after Arnold Schoenberg's 1911 treatise on tonal harmony, *Harmonielehre* refers not only to Schoenberg's book, but to the whole ferment of turn-of-the-century Viennese Expressionism. Although the outer movments still contain pulsating minimalist patterns, the central section ('The Anfortas Wound', a reference to the grail-questing King in Wagner's *Parsifal*) is one long anguished cry, embracing a sinuous, chromatic lyricism that seems more redolent of late Mahler or early Schoenberg than any of Adams's previous works. Coming after a fallow two-year period during which Adams experienced a painful creative block, *Harmonielehre* released the pent-up emotionality latent in his psyche. If this was minimalism, it was minimalism of explosive, sometimes hysterical, force.

Still, Adams does not always seek to craft a score as cathartic as *Harmonielehre*. In life as in art, he possesses an impudent, nose-thumbing streak that serves to balance his thoughtful, self-examining tendencies. That irreverent side occasionally bursts forth in works that are seemingly calculated to offend both friend and foe. In between two exalted creations like *Harmonium* and *Harmonielehre* came *Grand Pianola Music* (1981–2), as antic, parodistic, and downright campy a work as Adams has ever penned. 'Along with every dark, introspective, "serious" piece, there must come the Trickster, the garish, ironic wild card that threatens to lose me whatever friends the previous composition might have gained,' he wrote in 1989. 'I don't consciously choose to manipulate those polarities. It's more like being engaged in a kind of psychic balancing act, dark alternating with light, serene alternating with jittery, earnest alternating with ambiguous.'

Certainly *Grand Pianola Music* – like *American Standard* and *Lo-Fi* before it and *The Chairman Dances* (1985) and *Fearful Symmetries* (1988) after it – embodied the Trickster sprung to life. Scored for a chamber orchestra, three wordless sopranos, and two solo pianos, *Grand Pianola Music* provoked critical invective, particularly for its second movement. Titled 'On the Great Divide', it combines rippling, repeated minimalist patterns with that most simple-minded of pop-music chord progressions, tonic-dominant-tonic. As if that is not bad enough, Adams introduces 'The Tune', a banal melody that is whipped into increasingly perverse, grandiose climaxes. All the while, unrelated musical clichés – thumping marches, heroic Beethovenian piano arpeggios, ecstatic gospel harmonies – rub shoulders with delirious glee. 'Duelling pianos, cooing [female] sirens, Valhalla brass, thwacking bass drums, gospel triads and a Niagara of cascading flat keys all learned to cohabit as I wrote the piece,' Adams wrote. It is as if all the musical experiences of his youth had been thrown into one big pot and left to boil.

Had Adams lost his mind? Not at all. *Grand Pianola Music* was a way for him to reclaim forcibly the American popular culture he had loved as a young man, and what it lacked in subtlety it gained in adolescent brattiness. In 1987 he said that 'now I see it's the most thorough piece I've ever written about who I am musically. It has a real streak of vulgarity in it, full of the vernacular of American musical experience. With my name, what other kind of music am I supposed to write?'

And it was filled with one other element that had long been banished from contemporary music: humour. 'One of the truly tiresome things about contemporary music has been its incredibly dour, humourless quality,' Adams said. 'One of the things music can do better than any other art form is convey a sense of humour. As soon as you do that, you take yourself down off the heights of Parnassus.'

Now staring up at Parnassus from the gutter, Adams pondered his next move. Never much of a fan of the standard operatic repertory, he probably did not imagine that he would soon achieve world-wide fame by composing one of the first operas based on a contemporary subject. And his eclectic, post-minimalist vocabulary would find a natural home – wedded to the vivid drama of real-life music theatre.

In 1983 Adams was visiting his parents in New Hampshire when he met a young, fresh-out-of-Harvard wunderkind named Peter Sellars. Later in the 1980s Sellars would become notorious for taking Mozart's three most famous operas and setting them amid the urban blight and social ferment of contemporary America. But now he approached Adams with a novel idea – creating an opera based on Richard Nixon's historic 1972 meeting with Mao Tse-Tung. It would be called *Nixon in China*.

Adams reacted with amusement. 'I thought it would be ludicrous to make a familiar character like Nixon sing.' And he was sceptical of the idea of basing an opera on a contemporary subject. 'At that point I had been very deeply involved with Jung, and so my idea of opera was something that had to do with classical archetypes or myths. What I didn't realize was that *Nixon in China* was just exactly that – only that the myths, the archetypes, were famous political people of our own time.'

It took Adams a year to understand that not only was *Nixon in China* a brilliant idea, but that it might succeed in making opera meaningful to contemporary audiences. 'This is what opera should be doing,' he said in 1987. 'The movies, after all, do it all the time. Opera is so completely out of touch in this century; it has lost its relevance to our experience. We hardly need another opera based on a Shakespeare play or a Greek myth.' And if one turns from the dusty myths of the past to the mythic figures of the present, one can jar a complacent audience into a shock of recognition. 'If you mention

Hitler, or Donald Duck, or Marilyn Monroe, any number of buttons in our psyches are pressed.'

Or, for that matter, Richard Nixon. Indeed, a character like Nixon pressed so many buttons that most people assumed *Nixon in China* would be a broad satire, poking fun at the disgraced former President and his naïve First Lady. But Adams, Sellars, and their librettist, Alice Goodman, one of Sellars' Harvard classmates, were adamant that *Nixon in China* not be a political hatchet-job. Instead, they crafted a heroic, sympathetic opera framed in elegant rhyming couplets. 'The opera is about extraordinary human beings caught up in a tangle of personal and historical events,' said Adams. 'We've been calling the opera mythic, and I think it does contain a lot of myths. Nixon and the whole idea of self-righteousness and greatness and historical neces-

Nixon and Mao's famous handshake in Beijing, 1972, was an image that inspired Adams's opera *Nixon in China* (1987).

sity – those are all very classic American myths. Mao created his own myth by burying myths that were thousands of years old.'

It took Adams two years to compose *Nixon in China*, whose $80,000 commission fee was paid by the Houston Grand Opera, the Brooklyn Academy of Music, and, fittingly enough, Washington DC's Kennedy Center. By the time of its première in October 1987, the critic Michael Steinberg could state, without exaggeration: 'No American opera has ever been awaited with such excitement.'

Fortunately *Nixon in China* was an opera of such substance that it stood up to the onslaught of advance publicity. After a brooding introduction, filled with Glass-like repeated scales, the President's plane lands at the airport in Beijing – and out step Dick and Pat, dressed just as we remember them from news footage. They walk down the gangplank and, in one of those made-for-television moments, shake hands with Premier Chou En-Lai. (So realistic was this scene that the opening-night audience gasped audibly with delight.) Nixon's breathless, stuttering aria about the power of television, his meeting with Mao in the Chairman's book-lined study, the elaborate formal banquet for the visiting President: all seemed to leap off the front page and onto the opera stage.

Despite moments of pungent satire – such as the merciless portrayal of Henry Kissinger, or the flamboyant aria of Mao's wife – *Nixon in China* was an opera of greater subtlety than anyone had anticipated. During its last act the principal characters each lie on a narrow bed, and they have a chance to ruminate on their lives' accomplishments. For them, Adams wrote some of the most introspective and achingly poignant music he had ever penned.

No doubt there are still minimalist elements in *Nixon in China*, particularly in the orchestral accompaniment, which is filled with repetitive, Glass-like arpeggios. (Indeed, some Glass fans saw *Nixon* as a rip-off of their idol, despite the fact that *Nixon*'s vigorous narrative has nothing in common with the static tableaux of, say, *Satyagraha*.) But its lyrical vocal writing, so attuned to the cadences of American speech, avoided the pitfalls of Glass's text-setting. A new post-minimalist language now supported a clearly directionalized music-drama, heightening its emotions and lending its characters heroic aspirations.

After *Nixon in China*, Adams found himself an international celebrity. He was featured in *Time* and placed in *People*, alongside

Dolly Parton and Indira Gandhi. Not everybody liked *Nixon* – the *New York Times*'s Donal Henahan wrote that 'Mr Adams has done for the arpeggio what McDonald's did for the hamburger' – but the naysayers were in the minority. By the time the opera was aired on national television (with none other than the newscaster Walter Cronkite as host), the Adams/Sellars/Goodman team had moved on to a far more incendiary topic.

They based their second opera on the 1985 hijacking by Palestinian terrorists of the cruise ship *Achille Lauro*, and the murder of a wheel-chair-bound Jewish-American passenger, Leon Klinghoffer. But *The Death of Klinghoffer* (1991) went far beyond this particular event to examine, with nearly ritualistic sobriety, the tragic, timeless clash of two peoples, Arabs and Jews. And its music, filled with rich choral writing modelled on the Bach Passions, would go far beyond mini-malism – so much so that it falls outside the scope of this book.

Indeed, after *Nixon in China* it makes little sense to speak of Adams within a framework of minimalism. Today, minimalism is only one side of Adams's multi-faceted musical personality, and it is his ability to integrate styles, not merely juxtapose them, that seems most significant. More than any composer of his generation, Adams has achieved an accessible and genuinely American synthesis of serious classical ambition with the touch of the common man – a populism hardly heard since the heyday of Copland in the 1940s and Bernstein in the 1950s.

Adams has not been alone in taking the rhetoric of minimalism and making it serve the needs of a vital, post-modern music theatre. There is another American composer who has attempted a similar task, although she has approached it from a very different perspective. She cannot be ignored, but she tends to get slighted – simply because critics find her work so uncomfortably uncategorizable. Composer, singer, actor, choreographer, dancer, filmmaker and performance artist, hers is a protean talent that refuses to respect boundaries. Her name is Meredith Monk.

Monk emerged from the same lower-Manhattan artistic commu-nity that, a few years later, would nurture Reich and Glass. But her delight in blurring artistic categories extends back to her childhood in and around New York. Music was on her mother's side of the family: her great-grandfather had been a cantor in a Moscow synagogue, her

grandfather an operatic bass and conservatory director, and her mother a singer of operetta, popular songs and jingles. (Monk affectionately
recalls that her mother's voice was well-known from radio commer-
cials for Duz soap, Blue Bonnet margarine, Muriel cigars and Royal
pudding.) Monk could read music before she could read words, and
in 1946, when she was three years old, she began to study piano and
Dalcroze Eurythmics – a unified approach to arts education that
combines music with movement and improvisation. As a teenager,
her naturally flexible voice blossomed into a promising lyric soprano.

By the time she got to Sarah Lawrence College in New York's
wealthy northern suburbs, she was already practising a seamlessly
integrated approach to the arts. In her senior year she enrolled in a
performing-arts programme that combined composition, voice
lessons and opera workshop with choreography, theatre, and film
classes. After graduating in 1964 she moved to New York, and she
might have become just one of many multi-media performance artists
who crowded Soho in the mid-1960s – if not for her voice.

Monk is blessed with a three-octave range that would be the envy
of any operatic soprano, but it was not until shortly after her return to
Manhattan that she discovered its unique capabilities.

Left, the versatile
performance artist
Meredith Monk, laughing
during a rehearsal; *above,*
the circular lobby of the
Guggenheim Museum;
in progress is Monk's
'three-part cantata', *Juice,*
performed in the museum
in 1969.

*One day in 1965, while sitting at the piano, I had a revelation. I
realized that the voice could be as fluid as the spine, that it could have the
flexibility and range of the body. And that I could work with my voice to
develop my own instrument and my own vocabulary, just as I might do
choreography for my body. That same day I realized that the voice has all
these characters and landscapes within it – and in a flash I saw where I
would go from that point on.*

Where she went was down a path of her own devising. Monk
painstakingly created an absolutely unprecedented vocal technique.
She learned to use her voice to sing and dance, to moan and yodel,
to squeal, gurgle and whisper. She learned to evoke a panoply of
characters, from elderly women to little boys, from shrieking
ghosts to chattering animals and chanting priests. And, most
remarkably, she did so *entirely without words* – restricting herself
to swooping vocalise, nonsense syllables, and ritualistic incantations.
In 1978, after years of solo performance, she founded Meredith Monk

and Vocal Ensemble in order to teach a group of singers her 'extended vocal technique'.

That technique often seems to conjure up some alien culture, and it is tempting to hear in her music echoes of various non-Western styles – Inuit throat singing, Balkan nasality, Tibetan chanting. But she insists that she has hit upon these procedures purely by experimentation. 'By working with your own instrument, you actually come across gestures that are trans-cultural, and in certain ways you become part of the world vocal family. Sometimes I feel that I'm uncovering voices from an ancient past, that I'm almost a musical archeologist, unearthing spirits and memories of the human race.'

In Monk's work, talk of spirits does not seem out place. There is a beguiling enchantment and endearing ingenuousness to everything she does – a quality that might be described as naïve if that word didn't have pejorative connotations. Like a weaver of fables or legends she taps into a well-spring of myth that evokes a quasi-Jungian collective memory. It may be hard to pin down the meaning of her works, but one exists nonetheless.

Monk's enigmatic, non-narrative approach to music-theatre may owe a debt to Philip Glass and Robert Wilson's *Einstein on the Beach*. Her extended vocal techniques are typically supported by burbling keyboard patterns, built up from the repetition and transformation of brief melodic cells. (Although she, like Glass, despises the word minimalism, it would seem applicable to her instrumental textures – if not to her multiplicity of vocal styles.) And her striking combination of light, movement and staging, together with her suspended sense of time, are related to the static, elusive Wilsonian universe. Yet it would be wrong to suggest that Monk is an epigone, for it is she who has provided the model for younger singers (such as the performance artist Diamanda Galas) who seek to turn their voices to unconventional dramatic purposes.

Over the years Monk has created increasingly extended music-theatre works, some with a fragile narrative thread, and these she has labelled 'operas'. In *Book of Days* (released in 1988 as a black-and-white film, and later as a recording), the protagonist is Eva (played by Monk), a Jewish girl living in fourteenth-century Europe. Eva, who has disorienting visions of twentieth-century life, allows Monk to draw parallels between the Middle Ages, a time of plague, war, and religious persecution, and the modern age – a time of AIDS, nuclear

During her travels around the globe in Meredith Monk's opera *Atlas*, Alexandra (Monk) meets a lonely wailing spirit (Randall Wong).

annihilation, and racial strife. But Monk, typically, would rather suggest these contemporary political subjects than express them unequivocally. 'Because I work more like a poet than a prose writer, and since my form is basically a non-verbal one, I work more obliquely with that sort of political reality.'

In *Atlas* (1991), Monk brought together for the first time all her gifts – as composer, singer, choreographer, designer and director – under the umbrella of a genuine opera. Called 'an opera in three parts', *Atlas* was conceived for conventionally trained voices and instrumentalists, and so Monk had to frame her musical vocabulary in more traditional terms. *Atlas* was inspired by the life of the turn-of-the-century French explorer Alexandra David-Neel, the first Western woman to reach Tibet. In the opera, Alexandra and her travelling companions circle the globe, visiting an agricultural community, a rain forest, the Arctic ice and the Saharan desert. Along the way they endure a number of ordeals, making their voyage seem like a metaphor for spiritual growth. Finally they ascend to a timeless realm above the earth, a place of knowledge and beauty.

Clearly this is not the stuff of traditional opera. And Monk, like Reich, is neither a fan of the operatic repertory nor of the larger-than-life emotionality of the operatic stage. 'I love you!' she sang in a mocking quasi-operatic style. 'I just hate that. I never understand a word they're saying anyway. I feel that the voice itself is a language.'

So *Atlas* is that genuine rarity, an opera without a libretto. Using Monk's trademark vocal techniques, the eighteen singers produce a wordless lyricism of such elemental resonance that its meaning is clear. The effect is eerie: it is as if you are hearing a foreign language for the first time, and yet you understand every word. 'What I was interested in doing in *Atlas*,' said Monk, 'was to bypass discursive thought and go directly to the heart.'

In *Atlas*, as in Monk's earlier works, the vocal lines are supported by spare, luminously-textured instrumental parts. These simple, repeated melodies possess a haunting beauty, and they seem to grow and enlarge, almost unbidden, like the circling cry of a gull. It would not be unfair to describe Monk's instrumental writing as post-minimalist, since it takes the repetitive techniques and steady pulsation of minimalism, and infuses them with an increasingly expressive and personal style.

The work of both John Adams and Meredith Monk offers a glimpse of just how influential minimalism has become, and how malleable a style it can be. The composers of a second generation have taken the impersonal rigour of Reich and Glass and transformed it in ways that the pioneers could hardly have imagined. And now an even younger group of American composers has come onto the scene – one for whom Reich and Glass are like grandparents, and Adams is a spiritual father. In the work of Michael Torke (b. 1961), Aaron Jay Kernis (b. 1960), Julia Wolfe (b. 1958), David Lang (b. 1957), and Michael Gordon (b. 1956), elements of minimalism continue to inform an increasingly diverse musical style.

In less than forty years, minimalism has entered the history books and become a permanent part of the American musical vocabulary. If the importance of a style may be judged by its resilience, its influence, and its ability to withstand innumerable transformations, then minimalism has proved to be very important indeed.

7

A portrait of the archetypal
European minimalist, Dutch
composer Louis Andriessen

*It's earthy, it's physical, and that's contrary to
most American minimal music, which has a
very cosmic, California sound. In America there
is not enough angst. I'm much more aggressive, I
would say.*

Louis Andriessen

Europeans: Nyman, Andriessen, Pärt

Minimalism has often been viewed as a phenomenon born, nurtured, and developed in the USA. No doubt when it leaped to the public consciousness in the late 1960s it was associated with American composers like Terry Riley, Steve Reich and Philip Glass. But minimalism reached Europe very quickly – Reich and Glass, for instance, jointly made their first European tour in 1971 – and it soon became an international movement. Performed in rock-concert fashion by composer-led bands, drawing its inspiration from non-Western and popular music, this new minimalism seemed like a blast of brazenly American fresh air. And it suggested to many Europeans that there might be a way out of the dead-end of post-war serialism.

Several of these composers found the music of Riley, Reich and Glass positively revelatory. Indeed, it would not be an exaggeration to describe the reaction of the English composer Michael Nyman and the Dutch composer Louis Andriessen as akin to a creative epiphany, an experience so intense that it changed the direction of their compositional careers. Farther away in the former Soviet bloc, American minimalist music penetrated more slowly. But when it reached Arvo Pärt in Estonia and Henryk Górecki in Poland, an American musical language was made to sing with an overt (and very un-American) spirituality.

The man who has the unenviable distinction of being the first to apply the word minimalism to music, Michael Nyman might never have returned to composition if not for the new sounds he began hearing from America in the early 1970s. Considering his controversial status today – a composer who is immensely successful commercially, yet who has been wilfully marginalized by the classical-music establishment – it is important to remember that Nyman had an entirely respectable musical education.

Born in London on 23 March 1944, Nyman attended the Royal Academy of Music, where he studied piano, harpsichord, music history and composition (the latter with the Communist composer Alan Bush).

Next he went to King's College, London, where the musicologist and early-music specialist Thurston Dart introduced him to the glories of the English Renaissance and Baroque. (Nyman must have been struck by the way Henry Purcell, one of Dart's favourites, could combine simple repetition with structural ingenuity, and convey the loftiest passions in an accessible manner.) Dart also encouraged Nyman to pursue his nascent interest in folk music, and so in 1965 Nyman headed to Bucharest, where he carried out research in Romanian folk song.

By then Nyman had abandoned academia, but its legacy continued to fester. Years of schooling had left him with a compositional block so profound that from 1964 to 1976 he wrote virtually nothing. The cause of that block may be found not so much in internal creative forces as in external stylistic ones.

Michael Nyman, the man who first applied the word minimalism to music, working at the piano in 1993

When I was a student between '61 and '64 I wrote in a kind of a Hindemith-Shostakovich style. Then I came in contact with the

Manchester school – Maxwell Davies, Birtwistle, and Goehr – and it was
de rigeur *then not only to write serial music but to consider any other
music that wasn't serial as the music of idiots. You couldn't even show any
allegiance to Benjamin Britten! Everything was Darmstadt, this post-
Webern serial nonsense. I tried to write one serial piece, but I gave up.
And I didn't write a single note from '64 to '76, because I couldn't come to
terms with writing serial music.*

If he could not compose music, at least he could write about it.
For those twelve years, Nyman was a prolific critic, contributing regularly to *The Listener, The New Statesman,* and, especially, *The Spectator.*
It was there that Nyman, in a 1968 review of Cornelius Cardew's *The
Great Learning,* coined a new musical term – minimalism – which
he later described as 'a journalistic throwaway'. ('I don't mind going
to jail for six months; I'm the culprit,' he said with exasperation.) By
1974, Nyman's profound knowledge of the entire new-music scene
found expression in the book *Experimental Music: Cage and Beyond,*
still an unsurpassed view of post-war alternatives to the stifling
rhetoric of serialism. One of the options that Nyman discussed was
minimalism, a term that he now applied not only to Cardew but to
a group of American composers he had recently discovered – Young,
Riley, Reich, and Glass.

Nyman soon became a champion of American minimalism, and
even performed in England with Steve Reich and Musicians. But the
most important ramification of *Experimental Music* was that it allowed
Nyman to return to composition. It was almost as if, by so thoroughly
documenting the various stylistic paths available to an anti-serialist
composer, he had expiated his lingering bitterness – and found his
own voice.

In 1976 Harrison Birtwistle, then the director of music at
London's National Theatre, asked Nyman to arrange some eighteenth-
century Venetian gondolier's songs for a new production of Carlo
Goldoni's play *Il Campiello.* Nyman complied, scoring the old tunes
for a motley band that mixed medieval instruments (rebecs, sackbuts,
shawms) with those of popular music (banjo, bass drum and soprano
saxophone). The result was so noisy, so strident – and, to Nyman, so
intriguing – that he decided to preserve a version of the band as his
own ensemble, and to begin writing music for it.

And in a flash Michael Nyman became a card-carrying minimalist. 'When I started writing again in 1976 my musical style was kind of formed overnight, fully fledged, and obviously took note of minimalism rather than serialism,' he admitted. 'But because I was educated as a dyed-in-the-wool classicist (I was a musicologist), all my musical allegiances were toward tonal harmony and melody. Minimalism said "You can use tonal chords, you can use regular pulse," and of course that tied in with the kind of music I was listening to in the late sixties – Terry Riley, the Beatles, the Velvet Underground.'

Nyman immediately began composing for the new Michael Nyman Band, now shorn of its medieval instruments and armed with a heavily amplified line-up of winds (especially saxophones), brass, strings, keyboard and electric guitar. He was particularly delighted that minimalism had opened the door to popular music, a portal that serialism had slammed shut. 'It seems crazy to write a kind of music today which doesn't acknowledge the existence of pop music. For the Stockhausens and Birtwistles of this world to totally discard and scorn that music as a phenomenon seems nonsensical.'

But in most other ways Nyman's music was very different from American minimalism. Nyman was made uncomfortable by Reich and Glass's assimilation of African and Asian traditions, which he felt no Westerner could employ in good conscience. So Nyman's brand of minimalism, although indebted to the pulsating repetition of Reich and Glass, owes nothing to non-Western music. Indeed, his clearly directionalized, thumpingly climactic scores, and his familiar, archetypal chord progressions, come right out of the European classical heritage. As he explained:

That's one of the major differences I've always drawn as a critic and as a composer between the European minimalist and the American. Basically our tradition is European, and I get all my musical kicks and ideas from the European symphonic tradition. I'm certainly aware of the interconnections between what we're doing and various non-Western musics, but I've tried to not use them – partly because Ghanaian clothes are not my clothes, my clothes are Mozart, and I just feel the whole exploitative cultural-imperialism aspect of it rather severely. And maybe also because I tend to work in a very Westernized harmonic language.

Following page, a scene from Peter Greenaway's film The Draughtsman's Contract (1982), with music by Michael Nyman; the score first brought Nyman's music to public attention.

Nyman's detractors would argue that his language is not merely Western but positively parasitic. For what Nyman did in his works of the 1970s and 80s was to borrow the raw materials of classical music – a bass-line from Purcell, a melody from Schumann, or a chord progression from Mozart – and 'minimalize' them. Nyman took these shards of Western musical culture and submitted them to minimalist processes, including constant repetition, chugging pulse and contrapuntal layering. Then he clothed his creations in the raucous timbres of the Michael Nyman Band. The result, depending on whom you believe, is either blasphemy of the coarsest kind, or a compelling, post-modernist reinterpretation of the musical past.

In Re Don Giovanni (1977) takes a single chord progression from Mozart's opera and breaks it up into a series of constantly reiterated pulsations, as if the raw energy of rock had slammed into well-behaved eighteenth-century classicism. The film score for *The Draughtsman's Contract* (1982) is based entirely on the ground-basses and chaconnes of Purcell, and here Nyman's procedure does not violate Purcell's own: above the repeated bass-lines, which are now delivered with the punch of a rock band, Nyman crafts new melodies of sassy exuberance and, occasionally, throbbing poignance.

The Draughtsman's Contract was Nyman's first commercial success, and it cemented his relationship with the director Peter Greenaway. Between 1977 and 1990, Nyman and Greenaway worked on eighteen soundtracks (including ten films), one of the most fruitful collaborations in the history of modern cinema. *A Zed and Two Noughts* (1985), *Drowning by Numbers* (1987), *The Cook, The Thief, His Wife, and Her Lover* (1989) and *Prospero's Books* (1990) all showed that Nyman and Greenaway shared a similar artistic temperament. Filled with a Baroque love of excess, whether expressed in violence, sexuality, or sheer visual density, Greenaway's films combine orgiastic delirium with arcane rituals and litanies. For Greenaway, as for Nyman, the whole experience of history is available for re-examination. And for Greenaway, as for Nyman, that reinterpretation may have a shockingly rude exterior – but beneath lies a rational, formalistic structure that lends the flamboyant surface an unexpected coherence.

Nyman's most subtle work of the 1980s was his opera *The Man Who Mistook His Wife for a Hat* (1986). Based on a case study by the American neurologist Oliver Sacks, it tells the strange tale of an

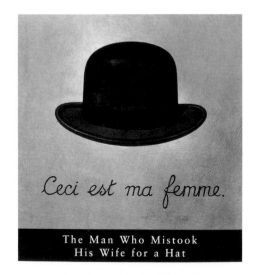

elderly 'Dr. P', who is able to see the environment around him but
can no longer make sense of what those images mean. Dr. P, a music
professor, associates songs with specific activities, and thus manages
to carry on with his daily life. In Nyman's opera those songs are from
Schumann's cycle *Dichterliebe*, and one particular melody, 'Ich Grolle
Nicht', becomes the subject of Nymanesque musical transformation.
The Man Who Mistook His Wife for a Hat, with its endlessly repeated
pulse and post-modern stew of historical references, owes a debt to
both Glass and Adams. But it exudes a refined tenderness that many
doubted Nyman possessed.

Millions of listeners around the world discovered that same vein of
poignancy in Nyman's soundtrack to Jane Campion's film *The Piano*
(1992). Nyman's score was written to be performed on camera by the
actress Holly Hunter, who plays Ada, a young woman newly arrived
in the remote bush of nineteenth-century New Zealand. Ada has
come from Scotland with her piano and young daughter; she has jour-
neyed to the South Pacific to consummate an arranged marriage. But

Ada, who is mute, can communicate only through her piano playing. 'Since Ada doesn't speak, the piano music doesn't simply have the usual expressive role but becomes the substitute for her voice,' Nyman wrote. 'The sound of the piano becomes her character, her mood, her expressions, her unspoken dialogues.'

Nyman, typically, turned to historical materials – in this case, old Scottish folk songs – but reinterpreted them in his own repetitive, minimalist fashion. He imagined that the music might have been composed by Ada herself, a quirky free spirit, and that gave him licence to pour his nineteenth-century sources into a very twentieth-century vessel. Some critics found the results anachronistic, even distracting from the visual narrative. But others were swept away by Nyman's newly sombre, expansive lyricism, one that seemed to capture the windswept mountains and stormy seascapes of New Zealand – as well as the smouldering passions trapped in Ada's soul.

The soundtrack of *The Piano* sold over 1.5 million copies, making Nyman into an international phenomenon rivalled only by Philip Glass. The Michael Nyman Band embarked on a worldwide tour, playing the music of *The Piano* in a concert version; yet another re-working of the same score turned up in *The Piano Concerto* (1993). Nyman, now increasingly eager to write for the orchestra, has no shortage of commissions for serious concert works. Yet he continues to lack the one thing he would seem to desire the most: the respect of the classical-music world.

Opposite, Ada (Holly Hunter) and her daughter Flora (Anna Paquin) are left stranded on a remote New Zealand beach, in this scene from Jane Campion's film *The Piano* (1992).

Dividing his time between a home in North London, an eighteenth-century farmhouse in the French Pyrenees, and touring with his band, Nyman certainly has achieved the commercial rewards of fame. But he wonders if is his popular success has rendered him artistically suspect. 'I've had to contend with a certain amount of envy and puffy-nosed disapproval,' he said in 1994. 'I can do a concert at Festival Hall in London and get a standing ovation, which doesn't happen much in new music. And there will always be a few sour-faced critics who sit around puzzled and angered and mystified.'

Perhaps there is something too facile, too overtly dependent, about Nyman's remodelling of historical clichés. But there can be no doubt that he has been influential. Without Nyman's model, it is unlikely that a younger post-minimalist like the English composer Steve Martland (born 1959) would be touring with the Steve Martland

Band, an amplified ensemble so strident that it makes Nyman's band look soft by comparison. (Martland's music, in fact, has provoked critical invective even harsher than Nyman's. One English classical critic suggested that Martland 'dig a large hole and bury his so-called music now and save posterity the trouble.')

Yet Martland studied not with Nyman but with Louis Andriessen, the Dutch composer whose provocative politics and controversial music have been scandalizing the classical-music establishment for decades.

Andriessen is often viewed as the quintessential European minimalist, a composer whose roots are as firmly planted in twentieth-century European modernism as in American minimalism. When one speaks with him, he is quick to mention that his idols are Johann Sebastian Bach and Igor Stravinsky. But it was his exposure to American minimalism that provided the catalyst for the development of his mature language.

The composer Louis
Andriessen, a guru for
rebellious young composers,
at home in Amsterdam

Born in Utrecht on 6 June 1939, Andriessen grew up hearing the music that was favoured by his father Hendrik (1892–1981), a composer and the organist at Utrecht Cathedral. Louis would sit next to

Hendrik in church, absorbing his father's improvisations as well as Bach's austere polyphony; at home, Hendrik preferred Stravinsky and French classicism to the emotive extremes of German Romanticism. Meanwhile, after the liberation of Holland in 1945, American jazz invaded Dutch soil – and Andriessen got to hear the bebop of Charlie Parker, and the big bands of Count Basie and Stan Kenton.

In 1957, just as the first wave of serial experimentation was sweeping across Europe, Andriessen entered the Royal Conservatory of Music in The Hague. Now he began studying with Kees van Baaren, Holland's first twelve-note composer. Recently he looked back on those days with evident pride. 'I must say that in 1958 I was one of the very first serial composers in Holland. I liked the strangeness of it. Totally different from the well-organized French world of my family, and so it was also a forbidden land, in a way!'

By the early 1960s Andriessen had abandoned serialism and plunged into the heady experimentation of the avant garde. From 1962 to 1964 he studied with Luciano Berio in Milan and Berlin, and got to know Pierre Boulez, Karlheinz Stockhausen, the Darmstadt school, and the American circle surrounding John Cage. But Andriessen, by now an impassioned Marxist, was increasingly distressed by the gulf between the avant garde's progressive ideals and its social elitism. And as he became enmeshed in the riots that erupted across the streets and campuses of Europe in the late 1960s, he understood that he needed a musical language that could communicate with a larger public. 'Seeing revolution on the streets, I realized that my choice [of musical style] had to involve the musicians and the world,' he said.

His first decision was to stop writing music for conventional ensembles, such as symphony orchestras.

At the time we said quite radical things, like orchestras are only important for the capitalists and the record companies, and so there was a very strong political reason to reject them. And I still think that's true, in fact. But there was also a musical reason. I was looking for another sound, a sound which had to do both with jazz and the classical avant garde.

So Andriessen founded his own 'democratic' ensemble, dedicated to eradicating the boundaries between 'high' and 'low' culture. Called

De Volharding (Perseverance), standing shoulder to shoulder in an aggressively militant fashion, Andriessen's band was equally at home at a street demonstration or in a concert hall.

But De Volharding needed an accessible and socially relevant music to play, and so it was fortunate that Andriessen had recently discovered American minimalism. The American composer Frederic Rzewski had brought the recording of Terry Riley's *In C* to Amsterdam in 1971, and Andriessen was immediately drawn to its repetitive jazz licks, its steady pulse, and its participatory, democratic approach to musical form. 'It brought highbrow and lowbrow together, which is exactly the way I thought, and still think, that music should go.'

Soon he heard the early pieces of Reich, and was so impressed that he organized performances of Reich's music at the Hague Conservatory. Andriessen must have sensed that Reich had a musical pedigree not that different from his own – a youth spent immersed in bebop and Stravinsky; a flirtation with serialism that left him with a predilection for structural rigour; and a musical style so radical that it demanded the formation of his own band. 'I was attracted to Steve's totally new approach to time in music, the non-developmental aspect, combined with the pop-oriented pulse. The music was open to many different kinds of influences from all over the world, and so I felt close to its ideology. And I recognized immediately very many open doors for the future.'

Right away, the music Andriessen composed for De Volharding betrayed his new immersion in American minimalism. But his brand of minimalism turned out to be as different from Reich's as Nyman's would later be. *De Staat* ('The State'; 1972–6), Andriessen's first large scale minimalist essay, defines a unique sonic universe of harsh unisons, loud dynamics, and a relentless rhythmic drive. And its strident timbre is far more uncompromising than the softer touch of American minimalism. 'It's earthy, it's physical, and that's contrary to most American minimalist music, which has a very cosmic, California sound,' Andriessen said with a chuckle. 'In America there is not enough angst! I'm much more aggressive, I would say.'

It is not just aggression that makes *De Staat* and its successor *De Tijd* ('Time'; 1979–81) so different from Reich and Glass. Andriessen's music possesses a gritty dissonance and a spiky chromaticism that speaks as much of European modernism – Stravinsky, Olivier

Messiaen, György Ligeti – as of minimalism. 'I am a European composer,' he stated unequivocally, 'and so even now I deal much more
than the Americans with chromaticism. My music is more complex
in general, it changes more often, and it's less diatonic in harmony.'

De Staat, with its raucous and pulsating combination of voices
and instruments, offers a startling anticipation of the later works of
John Adams. But *De Tijd* occupies a world unto itself. A setting of St
Augustine's musings on the nature of time, it aims, over its forty-
minute length, to suspend time's passing. Yet Andriessen, a European
to the core, cannot bear to embrace the non-developmental stasis of
Reich's music. In *De Tijd*, the eerie chromatic drones of the voices
and instruments are interrupted at increasingly frequent intervals by
crashes of metallic percussion, and so a clearly directionalized process
is at work. 'Although I minimalized the material, I developed it much
more than the Americans would,' he admitted.

Throughout the 1970s, Andriessen continued advocating on
behalf of American minimalism, and in 1976 he initiated a seminar
on minimalist music at the Hague Conservatory. From this project
emerged Andriessen's second band, Hoketus. Unlike the members of
De Volharding, who had been jazz musicians, the students in Hoketus
were devoted to rock – and brought with them the electric guitars and
percussion of popular music. 'Hoketus: they were just young dogs!'
said Andriessen with glee. 'But ideologically they were more or less
on the same line as De Volharding.'

For an unprecedented combination of De Volharding and
Hoketus, Andriessen wrote *De Stijl* (1984–5), scored for a snarling,
amplified assault of female voices, winds, brass, keyboards, electric
guitars, and 'heavy metal' percussion. (Andriessen, only half joking,
suggests that car bumpers would do nicely.) He calls the line-up 'the
terrifying twenty-first-century orchestra', and sees it as the ensemble of
the future.

De Stijl borrows its title from the artistic circle surrounding the
Dutch painter Piet Mondrian (1872–1944), whose abstract, geometric
canvases provide the basis for the music's arcane formal structure.
Although it was conceived as an independent work, *De Stijl* ultimately
became the third section of *De Materie* ('Matter'; 1984–9) – a large
four-part opera directed by none other than that master of non-narrative music-theatre, Robert Wilson.

More than any of Andriessen's major works, *De Stijl* makes explicit
the composer's fascination with popular culture. The piece rests upon
a funky, syncopated, and obsessively repeated 'disco bass', which is
first played by amplified keyboards and electric bass guitar – and
which dictates the course of the entire twenty-six-minute work.
Andriessen readily admits his debt to African-American music. 'You
know, I have a great sympathy for Motown; even in the 60s I thought
the Supremes were much better than the Beatles. During the last few
years, I've been buying Chaka Khan, Janet Jackson, Anita Baker,
Mariah Carey: all very good!'

With its unrelenting bass-line, its savage blasts of brass and winds,
its truly nasty crashes of percussion, and its violent propulsive force,
De Stijl would seem to be no less than an aesthetic manifesto. Indeed,
Andriessen's unique achievement has been his melding of the dissonance of European modernism, the repetition of American minimalism, and the power of pop. He still seems eager to eliminate the
barriers separating 'serious' and 'popular' culture. 'I think it's very
good to do that. I would again use the word democratic, the desire to
break down those borders. I think it's almost a duty, and not only for
composers. I hope that the future will bring us a better world in which
the difference between high and low, and rich and poor, is smaller
than it is now.'

Andriessen, who lives in Amsterdam, has become a veritable guru
for rebellious young composers. Attracted by his counter-cultural
image, his leftist politics, his contempt for mainstream classical-music
institutions, and his bracingly original musical synthesis, they flock to
Holland for study, conversation, and advice. Steve Martland's musical
style and aggressively anti-establishment attitude would not exist
without Andriessen; nor would New York's Bang On a Can Festival,
founded by three Andriessen disciples, David Lang, Julia Wolfe and
Michael Gordon. As he nears sixty, the Dutch composer must find
endless delight in all the trouble he continues to cause.

Both geographically and stylistically, Arvo Pärt stands apart from
the other composers in this book. Many would argue that his music
should not be included under the rubric 'minimalism'. More a neo-
medievalist than a minimalist, Pärt has crafted a body of work that
speaks of spiritual values in a language at once ancient and contemporary. In the midst of our aggressively secular age, Pärt's music radi-

Composition with Red, Yellow and Blue (1937) by the classical modernist Piet Mondrian, a member of the De Stijl movement. Mondrian's geometric canvases influenced the structure of Andriessen's synthesis of musical cultures, *De Stijl*.

ates a serene religiosity, one that refuses to become embroiled in the stylistic turmoil of late twentieth-century music.

But his serenity has been a hard-won virtue, and he bears the scars of battle not only in the furrows that crease his brow but in the sorrow that tinges his music. For Pärt, who was born in Paide, Estonia in 1935, grew up under the yoke of Soviet totalitarianism and state-sanctioned atheism.

When Pärt was eight years old, his mother and stepfather moved to a house that had a grand piano, and he was able to begin lessons. Since the middle register of the instrument was in a state of advanced decay, he had to restrict his musical investigations to the upper and lower regions. But he never heard orchestral music until he realized that recordings were occasionally broadcast over the loudspeakers in the town's main square. So Pärt, by now a teenager, would circle the plaza on his bicycle, hoping to capture some of the sound of the orchestra.

Pärt endured two years of compulsory service in the Soviet
military by working as a snare drummer in an army band. Only in
1958 was he able to begin a full-time study of music. He enrolled in
the conservatory in Tallinn, the Estonian capital, where he found
himself in the composition class of Heino Eller (1887–1970), a one-
time student of Glazunov. To earn a living, he got a job as a sound
director for the Estonian State Radio, a position that he held for ten
years – although he disliked most of the music that he was forced
to broadcast.

Eller, despite his roots in Russian late-Romanticism, must have
been an open-minded teacher, for he presided over Pärt's exploration
of post-war avant-garde techniques, which had just begun to filter
in from the West. Although Pärt's earliest works are tonal and show
the influence of Prokofiev and Shostakovich, by 1960 he had become
fascinated with serial technique. *Nekrolog* (1960), his first orchestral
piece, was also the first twelve-note composition written in Estonia.
Not suprisingly, it engendered harsh criticism from the Soviet cultural authorities, who regarded serialism as evidence of decadent, anti-
socialist tendencies. 'There was strong criticism from the highest
circles,' Pärt recalled in 1988. 'Nothing was considered more hostile
than so-called influences from the West, to which twelve-tone
music belonged.'

Pärt, always restless, did not remain satisfied with serialism
for long. His *Perpetuum Mobile* (1963) and Symphony No. 1 (1964),
although both serial works, display a density of texture and a savage
ferocity that aligns them with contemporary Polish sound-colourists
like Penderecki and Ligeti. And Pärt moved quickly away from strict
serial techniques and toward a more heterogeneous avant-garde vocabulary, combining elements of serialism with collage, quotation, and
even indeterminacy. His *Collage sur B-A-C-H* (1964) first transcribes
and then literally destroys a Bach sarabande; his Symphony No. 2
(1966) ends with a quotation from a children's piece by Tchaikovsky,
which is similarly assaulted by cacophony; his cello concerto *Pro Et
Contra* (1966) includes fragments of quasi-Baroque music. Clearly,
Pärt was searching for a path apart from serialism, but he had not yet
found his own way.

Pärt had graduated from the Conservatory in 1963, and by 1968
was able to leave his position at the radio and become a freelance

composer. Over the next decade he supported himself by writing music for some fifty films, a task that gave him more stylistic freedom than he had previously enjoyed. But it was not until he embraced his religious beliefs that he began to find his voice as a composer.

In 1968 Pärt composed a *Credo* for piano, chorus, and orchestra, a work that begins with the famous C major Prelude from Book 1 of Bach's *Well-Tempered Clavier*. Pärt progressively fragments and distorts the Bach until it achieves a screaming, hellish climax – and then he allows the simple purity of the Prelude to re-emerge triumphantly. It is as if Pärt were bidding farewell to the complexities of the avant garde, and re-embracing the power of unadulterated tonality.

The Soviet authorities would have agreed with this stylistic decision, but they could not countenance *Credo*'s overtly religious text, which begins with a bold declaration of faith: 'I believe in Jesus Christ.' As a result the work was banned, and Pärt was questioned regarding his political sympathies. "I didn't have political aims," he later recalled. 'Yet I was asked exactly this question about my political aims in this *Credo*.'

Partly because of his dispute with the authorities, and partly because he needed to rethink his stylistic posture, Pärt entered into his first (but hardly his last) period of creative silence. During the next two years he composed nothing, and he devoted his time to the study of medieval and Renaissance music. He examined the deceptively simple melodies of Gregorian chant, the austere polyphony of thirteenth-century Notre Dame organum, and the Renaissance masses and motets of Obrecht, Ockeghem, and Josquin. 'Gregorian chant has taught me what a cosmic secret is hidden in the art of combining two or three notes,' he said in 1988. 'That's something twelve-tone composers have not known at all.' Only once during the early 1970s did Pärt speak as a composer. His Symphony No. 3 (1971) is imbued with the pungent harmonies and complex counterpoint of fourteenth and fifteenth-century music. Pärt has called the symphony 'a joyous piece of music' but not yet 'the end of my despair and my search.'

That search continued for five more years, during which Pärt retreated to near-total compositional silence. He continued his immersion in the mysteries of medieval and Renaissance music, and began working with the Estonian early-music ensemble Hortus

Musicus. Sometime in the mid-1970s, he heard the music of Steve
Reich for the first time, and he must have been struck by the similari-
ties between the very old and the very new – both of which exhibited
a structural rigour and a severe reduction of musical materials.

In 1976, when Pärt returned to composition, he was a changed
man – a composer born again by virtue of his religious belief and
his faith in the power of the simplest possible musical expression.
Needless to say, his re-emergence was not exactly hailed by the authorities. By this time, the official Soviet composers had begun to
embrace, however cautiously, the serialism that Pärt had discarded
more than a decade earlier. 'And when about ninety per cent of them
were dodecaphonic, I created my tintinnabular style, and was declared
mad for the second time.'

Tintinnabulation comes from the Latin word for the ringing of
bells. Although Pärt's music of the late 1970s often includes the ar-
chaic sound of chiming bells, it is likely that he was speaking in more
metaphorical terms – that he intended to describe his new style as one
made up from the purest and most elemental musical ingredients.

But the cultural climate in the Soviet Union was as hostile to Pärt's
new simplicity as to his old spirituality, and by the mid-1970s he
longed for escape. Because Pärt's wife Nora is of Jewish descent, they
were able to apply for an exit visa, with Israel as the officially stated
destination. In January 1980 Pärt, his wife, and his children arrived
in Vienna, and by September 1981 they had moved to West Berlin.
Although technically an Austrian citizen, Pärt still makes his home in
the German capital.

It was only in 1984, when the first recording of Pärt's music was
released on the ECM label, that his work became known to a wider
audience. That album included three 'tintinnabular' works composed in 1977 – *Fratres*, *Cantus in Memory of Benjamin Britten*, and
Tabula Rasa – and it made a profound impression on critics and listeners around the world. But it only served to heighten the mystery
surrounding Arvo Pärt. Who was this man, whose long black beard,
high forehead, and sunken eyes made him look like a haunted Old
Testament prophet? And from what source did this timeless, seemingly unprecedented music spring?

Certainly it was not unreasonable to assume that these three
instrumental pieces were some East European offshoot of American

minimalism. For Pärt's new style, like minimalism, displayed an extreme reduction of musical means. Gone were the complexity, dissonance, and conflict of his early works. In their place was a musical language made up of the simplest, most elemental ingredients of tonality – scales, triads, and arpeggios – deployed with a static serenity, an ethereal clarity of texture, and a penchant for extended silences. If this was minimalism, it was of a sort far removed from the rapid-fire, kinetic, pop-influenced repetitions of Reich and Glass.

Fratres rests upon a droning open-fifth; above it, a slowly expanding melody swells to a climax and then recedes to nothingness. *Cantus* is even simpler: it consists of a descending minor scale, played by various string instruments at different but simultaneous tempos; interspersed is the tolling of a solitary funeral bell. *Tabula Rasa* resembles a Baroque concerto grosso for two solo violins and orchestra, and it is filled with Vivaldian arpeggios that break up a minor triad into busy figurations. But all three works share a fragile, hushed austerity that blurs the boundary between sound and silence – and all speak of an understated grief that transcends the bustle and novelty of our modern age.

Arvo Pärt discusses the performance of his *Miserere* with Paul Hillier of the Hilliard Ensemble, during rehearsals for the 1990 ECM recording of the work.

Pärt, a reclusive figure who refuses all requests for interviews, is given to elliptical statements that do more to obscure than illuminate his motivations. Yet his comments on his "tintinnabular" style are worth quoting, for they convey the sense of spiritual quest that must have characterized the search for this unique musical language.

'Tintinnabulation is an area I sometimes wander into when I am searching for answers – in my life, my music, my work,' he said in 1984. 'In my dark hours, I have the certain feeling that everything outside this one thing has no meaning. The complex and many-faceted only confuses me, and I must search for unity. What is it, this one thing, and how do I find my way to it? Traces of this perfect thing appear in many guises – and everything that is unimportant falls away. Tintinnabulation is like this. Here I am alone with silence. I have discovered that it is enough when a single note is beautifully played. This one note, or a silent beat, or a moment of silence, comfort me. I work with very few elements – with one voice, with two voices. I build with the most primitive materials – with the triad, with one specific tonality. The three notes of a triad are like bells. And that is why I called it tintinnabulation.'

In 1987, when ECM released Pärt's second album, *Arbos*, it became clear that the previous disc of instrumental music had created a false impression. Rather than being inspired by the stridently secular minimalism emanating from America, Pärt's aesthetic was clearly religious in orientation, informed by his study of Western chant and his involvement with the rituals of the Russian Orthodox Church. Its reduction of means and seeming simplicity might make it appear mini-malist. But its desire to wring the maximum of expressive content from every single note – and its burning spirituality – left minimalism behind.

In recent years, Pärt has devoted himself almost entirely to the composition of sacred vocal music in Latin. His three largest works of the 1980s – *Passio* (1982), Stabat Mater (1985), and *Miserere* (1989) – are all related to the Passion, a subject ideally suited to his music's tragic demeanour. Yet unlike nineteenth-century Romantics or twentieth-century Expressionists, Pärt treats the Passion in a severely restrained, nearly disembodied manner, a non-illustrative approach to text-setting that is far closer to the Middle Ages than to the modern age. It's not that this music is unemotional, but that its poignancy accumulates gradually – from the slow, inexorable repetition of deceptively simple, severely ritualistic formal structures.

Consider, for instance, the seventy-one-minute *Passio*, a setting of the Passion according to St. John. So austere is Pärt's realization that, in the words of critic Peter Davis, it 'makes Bach's familiar Eastertide version sound like an overheated Puccini melodrama.' Pärt, in fact, does all he can to neutralize the drama inherent in the New Testament text. The narrative provided by the Evangelist is given not to a soloist but to a quartet of voices who intone the text with stark simplicity, their rhythmic unison reminiscent of chant and early organum. They in turn are joined by four solo instruments who move in tandem with (not in counterpoint to) the voices. Jesus is a bass who is accompanied by the organ; Pilate is a tenor; the crowd scenes are, not surprisingly, given to a full chorus.

But there is neither dramatic conflict nor directionalized climax as the work progresses; it merely unfolds, in a methodical and contemplative alternation of forces. Although the translucent musical language – consisting of sombre minor triads and scales, and constant, equal-valued rhythms – might at first seem quasi-medieval, Pärt throws in an occasional gritty dissonance to remind us that this is a twentieth-century work. At the very end, the chorus returns for a concluding chorale set to the text 'You who have suffered for us, have mercy on us.' For the first time Pärt makes use of the major mode, and the voices radiate an aura of ethereal transcendence. It is a stunning capstone to a piece with no precedent in twentieth-century music.

Pärt cares little for fame or fortune, preferring to live quietly and simply in a leafy suburb of Berlin, where he spends time with his family, attends services at the Russian Orthodox Church, and composes in absolute isolation. His adoption of a 'tintinnabular' idiom occurred honestly and after much struggle; the fact that it has turned out to be successful commercially would seem irrelevant.

But Pärt is not alone in having wrestled with external political repression and internal spiritual crisis. Nor is he alone in having combined elements of minimalism with the fervent mysticism of the Orthodox ritual and the timeless utterances of East European folk music. A similar synthesis may be found in the works of the Polish composer Henryk Górecki (especially the immensely successful Symphony No. 3 [1976]), the Georgian composer Giya Kancheli, and the English composer John Tavener. Indeed, a whole new stylistic umbrella – 'spiritual minimalism' – has been coined to set these composers apart from their more hyperactive American brethren.

Still, it is Pärt's achievement that is the most astonishing. His music seems neither of this era nor, in some ways, of this world. It drifts in quietly from another sphere, making use of virtually primordial materials. It offers us a moment of repose, it soothes our sorrow, and it suggests the possibility of transcendence. Then it fades away, rising upwards to the heights from where it came. Whether or not it is really minimalism seems beside the point.

Classified List of Works

The lists which follow (ordered alphabetically by composer) are based primarily on material provided by the composers' publishers Boosey & Hawkes (Reich, Adams, Andriessen), Dunvagen Music/G. Schirmer (Glass), Chester (Nyman) and Universal/European-American (Pärt). For La Monte Young, Terry Riley and Meredith Monk, information provided by the composers was used to supplement the work-lists found in the *New Grove Dictionary of American Music* (London and New York, Macmillan, 1986). The lists for Reich and Glass are reasonably comprehensive, while those for the other composers are highly selective. Although the works are listed according to categories (Music Theatre, Orchestral, Chamber/Instrumental, Vocal/Choral, etc.), in some cases (e.g. Meredith Monk) the categorization breaks down entirely, as the works themselves blur the boundaries between media. Dates given in parentheses are those of composition; 'fp' denotes first public performance, details of which are given when made available by the publisher.

John Adams

Opera

Nixon in China, opera in three acts, libretto by Alice Goodman (1987). fp Houston, Texas, 22 October 1987

The Death of Klinghoffer, opera in two acts, text by Alice Goodman (1990). fp Brussels, 19 March 1991

Orchestral/Vocal with Orchestra/Large Ensemble

Shaker Loops, for string orchestra (1978, revised 1983). fp 26 April 1983

Common Tones in Simple Time (1979). fp San Francisco, California, 28 January 1980

Harmonium, for chorus and orchestra, words by John Donne and Emily Dickinson (1980–1). fp San Francisco, California, 15 April 1981

Grand Pianola Music, for wind ensemble, three percussion, two pianos, three amplified women's voices (1981–2). fp San Francisco, California, 26 February 1982

Harmonielehre (1984–5). fp San Francisco, California, 21 March 1985

The Chairman Dances ('Foxtrot for Orchestra') (1985). fp Milwaukee, Wisconsin, 31 January 1986

Short Ride in a Fast Machine (1986). fp Great Woods, Mansfield, Massachusetts, 13 June 1986

Tromba lontana (1986). fp Houston, Texas, 4 April 1986

Fearful Symmetries, for orchestra or chamber orchestra (1988). fp New York, 29 October 1988

Eros Piano, for piano and orchestra or chamber orchestra (1989). fp London, 24 November 1989

The Wound-Dresser, for baritone and orchestra or chamber orchestra, words by Walt Whitman (1989). fp St Paul, Minnesota, 24 February 1989

El Dorado, for orchestra (1991). fp San Francisco, California, 11 November 1991

Chamber Symphony, for fifteen instrumentalists (1992). fp The Hague, 17 January 1993

Violin Concerto, for violin and orchestra (1993). fp Minneapolis, Minnesota, 19 January 1994

Chamber/Instrumental

Phrygian Gates, for piano (1977). fp San Francisco, California, 17 March 1978

Shaker Loops, for string septet (1978). fp San Francisco, California, 13 December 1978

John's Book of Alleged Dances, for string quartet and foot-controlled sampler (1994). fp Escondido, California, 19 November 1994

Louis Andriessen

Opera/Music Theatre

De Materie ('Matter'), stagework for soprano and tenor soloists, two speakers, eight voices and large ensemble, in collaboration with Robert Wilson (1985–8). fp Amsterdam, 1 June 1989

Rosa, opera in collaboration with Peter Greenaway (1994). fp Amsterdam, 1994

Orchestral/Large Ensemble

Anachronie 1, for orchestra (1966–7). fp Rotterdam, 18 January 1968

De Staat, for four women's voices and large ensemble, words from Plato's *Republic* (1972–6). fp Amsterdam, 28 November 1976

Hoketus, for two groups of five instrumentalists (1975–7). fp The Hague, 31 May 1976

De Tijd ('Time'), for female choir and large ensemble, words from St Augustine's *Confessions*, Vol. II, Chapter II (1980–1). fp The Hague, 1 June 1981

De Snelheid ('Velocity'), for large ensemble (1982–3), revised 1984). fp San Francisco, California, 11 January 1984

De Stijl (*De Materie*, third section), for four women's voices, female speaker and large ensemble, words by Dr M. H. J. Schoenmaekers and M. van Domselaer-Middelkoop (1984–5). fp Amsterdam, 9 June 1985

M is for Man, Music, Mozart, for jazz singer and large ensemble, music for the video by Peter Greenaway (1991). fp Utrecht, 22 September 1991

Philip Glass

The following may be considered a complete list of works, although it omits juvenilia (in Glass's case, that means all music composed prior to 1965). PGE denotes works written for the Philip Glass Ensemble.

Opera/Music Theatre/Mixed-media

Einstein on the Beach, opera in four acts, for PGE, vocal soloists and chorus, created with Robert Wilson (1975–6). fp Avignon, 25 July 1976

Dance, for PGE, a collaborative work with choreographer Lucinda Childs and sculptor-painter Sol LeWitt (1979)

A Madrigal Opera, for six voices, violin and viola (1980). fp Netherlands, 1980

Satyagraha, opera in three acts for orchestra, chorus and soloists (1980). fp Rotterdam, 5 September 1980

The Photographer, for chamber orchestra, music-theatre piece written with director-author Rob Malasch (1982). fp Amsterdam, June 1982

the CIVIL warS (Rome Section), opera with prologue and three scenes, devised with Robert Wilson (1983). fp Rome, 22 March 1984

Akhnaten, opera in three acts for orchestra, chorus and soloists (1984). fp Stuttgart, 24 March 1984

The Juniper Tree, opera in two acts for chamber orchestra, small chorus and soloists, written with composer Robert Moran and author Arthur Yorkins, based on the tale by the Brothers Grimm (1984). fp Cambridge, Massachusetts

Music for *Company* by Samuel Beckett, for string quartet (1984)

A Descent into the Maelstrom, for PGE (1985)

In the Upper Room, dance work written for Twyla Tharp (1986)

The Making of the Representative for Planet 8, opera in three acts, libretto by Doris Lessing (1986). fp Houston, Texas, 1986

1000 Airplanes on the Roof, opera (1988). fp Vienna, 15 July 1988

The Fall Of The House of Usher, opera (1988). fp Cambridge, Massachusetts, 18 May 1988

Hydrogen Jukebox, opera written with poet Allen Ginsberg (1990)

Music for Jean Genet's play *The Screens* (1990)

Music for Mysteries and What's So Funny, written by David Gordon (1991)

White Raven, opera devised with Robert Wilson, for soloists, chorus and orchestra (1991)

The Voyage, opera, libretto by David Henry Hwang (1992). fp New York, 12 October 1992

Orphée, opera based on the film by Jean Cocteau (1993)

Woyzeck, music for the play by Georg Büchner (1993)

La Belle et la Bête, opera synchronized with the film by Jean Cocteau (1994)

Orchestral

the CIVIL warS (Cologne section), for orchestra with optional mixed chorus (1984). fp Cologne, January 1984

The Olympian, for chorus and orchestra (1984). fp Los Angeles, California, 1984

Concerto for violin and orchestra (1987). fp New York, 5 April 1987

The Light (1987). fp Cleveland, Ohio, 7 February 1988

The Canyon, for orchestra (1988). fp Rotterdam, 18 October 1988

Itaipu, for chorus and orchestra (1989). fp Atlanta, Georgia, 2–4 November 1989

Concerto Grosso (1992)

'Low' Symphony, based on themes from David Bowie's *Low* (1992)

Symphony No. 2 (1994). fp New York, 14 October 1994

Symphony No. 3 (1994)

Chamber/Instrumental

Play, incidental music for *Play* by Samuel Beckett, for two soprano saxophones (1965)

String Quartet No. 1 (1966)

In Again Out Again, for two pianos (1967)

Music in the Form of a Square, for two flutes (1967)

One Plus One, for amplified tabletop (1967)

Strung Out, for solo amplified violin (1967)

Two Pages, for electric keyboards (1968)

Music in Contrary Motion, for PGE (1969)

Music in Fifths, for PGE (1969)

Music in Similar Motion, for PGE (1969)

Music with Changing Parts, for PGE (1970)

Another Look at Harmony, Parts 1 and 2, for PGE (1975)

Glassworks, for PGE (1981), recording for CBS Masterworks

String Quartet No. 2, from music for *Company* by Samuel Beckett (1984)

String Quartet No. 3, from film score *Mishima* (1985)

Metamorphosis for Piano (1989)

String Quartet No. 4 ('Buczak') (1989)

String Quartet No. 5 (1991)

Vocal

Songs from Liquid Days, song cycle with lyrics by Laurie Anderson, David Byrne, Paul Simon and Suzanne Vega (1985)

Film Music

North Star, music for the documentary film *Mark Di Suvero, Sculptor* by François de Menil and Barbara Rose (1977)

Koyaanisqatsi, music for wind ensemble, solo bass, chorus and orchestra, for the film by Godfrey Reggio (1982)

Mishima, music for the film written by Paul and Leonard Schrader, directed by Paul Schrader (1984)

Powaqqatsi, music for the film directed and produced by Godfrey Reggio (1987)

The Thin Blue Line, music for the Errol Morris film (1988). fp Cambridge, Massachusetts, 18 May 1988

Anima Mundi, music for the film by Godfrey Reggio (1992)

A Brief History of Time, music for the film by Errol Morris (1992)

Meredith Monk

Vocal/Choral/Mixed-media

Juice: A Theater Cantata, for eighty-five voices, Jew's harp and two violins (1969)

Vessel: An Opera Epic, for seventy-five voices, electric organ, dulcimer and accordion (1971)

Education of the Girlchild: An Opera, for six voices, electric organ and piano (1972–3)

Quarry: An Opera, for thirty-eight voices, two pump organs, two soprano recorders and tape (1976)

Recent Ruins, for fourteen voices, tape and cello (1979)

Dolmen Music, for six voices, piano, violin, cello and percussion (1979–81)

Turtle Dreams, for four voices and two electric organs (1980–1)

Specimen Days, for fourteen voices, piano and two electric organs (1981)

The Games, for sixteen voices, synthesizer, keyboards, Flemish bagpipes, bagpipes, Chinese horn and Rauschpfeife (1983)

Do You Be, for ten voices, two pianos, synthesizer, violin and bagpipes (1987)

The Ringing Place, for nine voices (1987)

Book of Days, for twelve voices, synthesizer, cello, bagpipe, hurdy gurdy, piano and hammered dulcimer (recorded version, 1990); for ten voices, cello, shawm, synthesizer, hammered dulcimer, bagpipe and hurdy gurdy (film score, 1988)

Facing North, for two voices and tape (1990)

Atlas: An Opera In Three Parts, for eighteen voices and ensemble (1991)

Custom Made, 1. *Steppe Music*, for solo piano; 2. *Volcano Songs*, for two voices; 3. *St. Petersburg Waltz*, for solo piano and two voices; 4. *New York Requiem* ('Blues for Tom'), for solo piano and voice (1993)

Michael Nyman

Music Theatre

The Man Who Mistook His Wife for a Hat, chamber opera for soprano, tenor, baritone and ensemble, libretto by Christopher Rawlence, based on the case study by Oliver Sacks (1987)

Letters, Riddles and Writs, TV opera for mezzo-sopran (or counter-tenor), bass and ensemble, words by Jeremy Newson after Mozart (1991). fp 10 November 1991 (on screen); London, 24 June 1992

Orchestral

Where the Bee Dances, concerto for soprano saxophone and chamber orchestra (1991). fp Cheltenham, 13 July 1991

MGV (Musique à Grande Vitesse) (1993). fp Lille, 26 September 1993

The Piano Concerto (1993). fp Lille, 26 September 1993

Vocal

Six Celan Songs, for low female voice and ensemble (1990). fp Amsterdam, 1 February 1992

Ariel Songs (from *Prospero's Books*), for soprano (or mezzo-soprano) and ensemble, words by Shakespeare (1990–1). fp London, 1991

Self-Laudatory Hymn of Inanna and Her Omnipotence, for counter-tenor and viols, words from Ancient Near Eastern texts relating to the Old Testament, translated by S. N. Kramer (1992). fp London, 11 June 1992

Chamber/Instrumental

In Re Don Giovanni, for ensemble (1977). fp London, 1977

Think Slow, Act Fast, for two panpipes, two alto saxophones, two pianos, two bass guitars and two percussionists (1981). fp London, 1981

I'll Stake My Cremona to a Jew's Trump, for electronically modified violin and viola and simultaneous singing (1983). fp Leicester, 1983

String Quartet No. 1 (1985). fp London, 3 November 1985

Zoo Caprices, for solo violin (1985). fp Paris, 8 April 1986

Taking a Line for a Second Walk, for two pianos (1986). fp London, 1986

String Quartet No. 2 (1988). fp London, 15 September 1988

Shaping the Curve, for soprano saxophone and piano (1990). fp 1990

String Quartet No. 3 (1990). fp London, 16 February 1990

Masque Arias, for brass quintet (1991). fp Cambridge, 1991

The Convertibility of Lute Strings, for harpsichord solo (1992). fp London, 17 November 1992

For John Cage, for ten-piece brass ensemble (1992). fp Ashford, 16 November 1992

Goodbye Frankie, Goodbye Benny, for violin, cello and piano (1992). fp Cheltenham, 14 July 1992

Film Music

1–11, music for the film directed by Peter Greenaway (1977)

A Walk Through H, music for the film directed by Peter Greenaway (1977)

Vertical Features Remake, music for the film directed by Peter Greenaway (1978)

The Falls, music for the film directed by Peter Greenaway (1980)

The Draughtsman's Contract, music for the film directed by Peter Greenaway (1982). fp Edinburgh, 1983

A Zed and Two Noughts, music for the film directed by Peter Greenaway (1985). fp London, 1985

Drowning by Numbers, music for the film directed by Peter Greenaway (1988). fp Paris, 1988

The Cook, The Thief, His Wife, and Her Lover, music for the film directed by Peter Greenaway (1989)

Prospero's Books, music for the film directed by Peter Greenaway (1990)

The Piano, music for the film directed by Jane Campion (1992)

Arvo Pärt

Orchestral

Nekrolog, Op. 5 (1960)

Perpetuum Mobile, Op. 10 (1963)

Collage sur B-A-C-H, for strings, oboe, harpsichord and piano (1964)

Symphony No. 1 (1964)

Pro Et Contra, concerto for cello and orchestra (1966)

Symphony No. 2 (1966)

Credo, for piano, chorus and orchestra (1968). fp Edinburgh, 9 October 1981

Symphony No. 3, for orchestra (1971)

Fratres, for string orchestra and percussion (1977, revised 1991). fp Stockholm, 29 April 1983

Tabula Rasa, double concerto for two violins (or violin and viola), string orchestra and prepared piano (1977). fp Tallinn, 1977

Cantus in Memory of Benjamin Britten, for string orchestra and bell (1980). fp London, September 1979

Summa, for string orchestra (1980–90)

Festina Lente, for string orchestra and harp ad lib (1988, revised 1990). fp Helsinki, 5 May 1989

Fratres, for violin, string orchestra and percussion (1977–92). fp Perth, Australia, 13 February 1993

Vocal/Choral

An Den Wassern Zu Babel Sassen Wir Und Weinten, Psalm 137 for voices and instruments (1976–84, revised 1994). fp Witten, 28 April 1984

Sarah Was Ninety Years Old, for three voices (1977). fp New York, 10 March 1984

De Profundis, for men's chorus, percussion ad lib and organ (1980). fp Kassel, 25 April 1981

Passio Domini nostri Jesu Christi secundum Joannem, for tenor, bass, vocal quartet, instrumental quartet and organ (1982). fp Munich, 28 November 1982

Es Sang Vor Langen Jahren, motet for alto (or countertenor), violin and viola (1984)

Te Deum, for three choirs, piano, tape (aeolian harp) and strings (1984–5, revised 1986). fp Cologne, 19 January 1985

Stabat Mater, for soprano, alto, tenor, violin, viola and cello (1985). fp Lockenhaus, 9 July 1985

Magnificat, for chorus *a cappella* (1989). fp Stuttgart, 23 May 1990

Miserere, for soloists, chorus, ensemble and organ (1989, revised 1990). fp Rouen, 17 June 1986

Summa, for chorus or solo voices *a cappella* (1980–90). fp Witten, 27 April 1984

Berliner Messe, for chorus or soloists with organ or string orchestra (1990, revised 1991). fp Berlin, 24 May 1990

Litany: Prayers of St John Chrysostom for Each Hour of the Day and Night, for solo, choir and orchestra (1994). fp Eugene, Oregon, 24 June 1994

Chamber/Instrumental

Für Alina, for piano (1976)

Fratres, for chamber ensemble (1977). fp Vienna, 8 February 1982

Fratres, for cello and piano (1977). fp Hitzacker, 30 July 1989

Fratres, for violin and piano (1977–80). fp Salzburg, 17 August 1981

Fratres, for four, eight or twelve cellos (1977–83). fp Berlin, 18 September 1982

Fratres, for string quartet (1977–85). fp London, 12 June 1986

Arbos, for eight brass and percussion (1977–86). fp Aptos, California, 27 July 1987

Summa, for violin, two violas and cello (1980–90)

Summa, for string quartet (1980–91)

Steve Reich

The following may be considered a complete list of works, although it omits juvenilia (in Reich's case, that means most music composed prior to 1965).

Music Theatre

The Cave, documentary video music-theatre work in three acts, words from the Torah, plus Rabbinical commentary, the Koran and documentary material (1990–3). fp Vienna, 16 May 1993

Orchestral/Vocal with Orchestra/Large Ensemble

Music for a Large Ensemble (1978). fp Netherlands, June 1979

Eight Lines (1979, revised 1983), revised version of *Octet*. fp New York, 10 December 1983

Variations for Winds, Strings and Keyboards (1979, revised 1980). fp San Francisco, California, 14 May 1980

Tehillim, for voices and ensemble, words (in Hebrew) from Psalms 19, 34, 18, 150 (1981). fp Stuttgart, June 1981 (1st and 2nd movements); Cologne, 20 September 1981 (complete work)

The Desert Music, for chorus and orchestra, text by William Carlos Williams (1982–4). fp Cologne, 17 March 1984

Three Movements, for orchestra (1986). fp St Louis, Missouri, 3 April 1986

The Four Sections, for orchestra (1987). fp San Francisco, California, 7 October 1987

Chamber/Instrumental

Pitch Charts, variable instrumentation (1963)

Music, for three or more pianos (or piano and tape) (1964)

Reed Phase, for soprano saxophone and tape (1966)

Piano Phase, for two pianos (or two marimbas) (1967)

Violin Phase, for violin and tape (or four violins) (1967)

Pendulum Music, for three or more microphones, amplifiers, loudspeakers and performers (1968)

Four Log Drums, for phase-shifting pulse gate and log drums (1969)

Pulse Music, for phase shifting pulse gate (1969)

Four Organs, for four electric organs and maracas (1970)

Phase Patterns, for four electric organs (1970)

Drumming, for four pairs of tuned bongos, three marimbas, three glockenspiels, two female voices, whistling and piccolo (1971). fp New York, December 1971

Clapping Music, for two performers clapping (1972)

Music for Mallet Instruments, Voices and Organ (1973). fp New York, 16 May 1973

Music for Pieces of Wood, for five pairs of tuned claves (1973)

Six Pianos (1973). fp New York, 16 May 1973

Music for 18 Musicians (1974–6). fp New York, 24 April 1976

Octet (1979). fp Frankfurt, 21 June 1979

Vermont Counterpoint, for flute and tape (1982). fp New York, 1 October 1982

Sextet, for percussion and keyboards (1984, revised 1985). fp Paris, 19 December 1984

New York Counterpoint, for clarinet and tape (1985). fp New York, 20 January 1986

Six Marimbas (1986), version of *Six Pianos*. fp New York, 20 April 1987

Electric Counterpoint, for electric guitar and tape (1987). fp New York, 5 November 1987

Different Trains, for string quartet and tape (1988). fp London, 2 November 1988

City Life, for Ensemble InterContemperain (1995). fp Metz, 7 March 1995

Tape

The Plastic Haircut, film music (1963)

It's Gonna Rain (1965). fp San Francisco, California, January 1965

Oh Dem Watermelons, film music, reworked songs of Stephen Foster (1965)

Come Out (1966). fp New York, April 1966

Melodica (1966). fp New York, June 1966

My Name is, text score, for three or more recorders, performers and audience (1967)

Slow Motion Sound, text score (1967)

Terry Riley

Chamber/Instrumental

Trio, for violin, clarinet and cello (1957)

String Quartet (1960)

String Trio (1961)

Mescalin Mix, for tape (1962–3)

Keyboard Studies (1963)

Dorian Reeds, for wind, brass, strings, unspecified instruments and tape loops (1964)

In C, for unspecified instruments (1964)

Poppy Nogood and the Phantom Band, for soprano saxophone, electric keyboard and tape delay (1967)

A Rainbow in Curved Air, for electric keyboard, dumbak and tambourines (1968)

Shri Camel, for electric organ and tape delay (1976)

G-Song, for voice, string quartet and synthesizer (originally for electric keyboard) (1981)

Sunrise of the Planetary Dream Collector, for voice, synthesizer and string quartet (1981) (original version for electric keyboard, 1973)

Cadenza on the Night Plain, for string quartet (1984)

Salome Dances for Peace, for string quartet (1986)

La Monte Young

Electronic/Mixed-media

2 Sounds (1960). fp New York, 31 January 1961

Poem for Tables, Chairs, Benches, Etc., for any sound sources (1960). fp Los Angeles, California, 6 February 1960

The Tortoise, His Dreams and Journeys, for voices, various instruments, electric drones (1964–)

Map of 49's Dream the Two Systems of 11 Sets of Galactic Intervals Ornamental Lightyears Tracery, for voices, various instruments, sine wave drones (1966–). fp Pasadena, California, 28 January 1968

Chamber/Instrumental

Five Small Pieces for String Quartet (1956). fp Los Angeles, California, 2 November 1956

For Brass, for two horns, two trumpets, two tubas (1957). fp Palo Aalto, California, 3 May 1958

For Guitar (1958). fp New York, 7 December 1979

Trio for Strings (1958). fp San Francisco, California, 29 November 1960

Studies I, II (incomplete), *III*, for piano (1959). fp Los Angeles, California, 25 February 1959 (I)

Vision, for eleven instruments (1959). fp Berkeley, California, 2 December 1959

Arabic Numeral (Any Integer), to Henry Flynt, for gong and piano (1960). fp New York, 14 May 1961

Death Chant, for male voices and carillon (1961). fp Düsseldorf, 16 June 1962

The Second Dream of the High-Tension Line Stepdown Transformer from the Four Dreams of China, any instruments that can sustain four-note groups in just intonation (1962). fp North Brunswick, New Jersey, 19 May 1963

The Well-Tuned Piano, for prepared piano (1964–). Realizations include Rome, 3 June 1974; New York, 2 April 1975; New York, 25 October 1981

Action and Text Works

Compositions 1960, Nos. 2–6, 9, 10, 13, 15 (1960)

Piano Pieces for David Tudor, Nos. 1–3 (1960)

Compositions 1961, Nos. 1–29 (1961). fp Cambridge, Massachusetts, 31 March 1961

Further Reading

Dreier, R. 'Minimalism', in H. Wiley Hitchcock and S. Sadie (eds.) *The New Grove Dictionary of American Music* (London and New York, Macmillan, 1986)

Glass, P. *Music by Philip Glass* (New York, Harper & Row, 1987)

Hitchcock, H. W. *Music in the United States* (3rd edition: Englewood Cliffs, New Jersey, Prentice-Hall, 1988)

Mertens, W. *American Minimal Music* (London, Kahn & Averill, 1983)

Nyman, M. *Experimental Music: Cage and Beyond* (London, Studio Vista, 1974)

Page, T. 'Framing the River: A Minimalist Primer', in *High Fidelity*, November 1981

Reich, S. *Writings About Music* (Halifax, Nova Scotia, The Press of the Nova Scotia College of Art and Design, 1974)

Reich, S. and Korot, B. *The Cave* (London and New York, Hendon Music/Boosey & Hawkes, 1993)

Rockwell, J. *All American Music: Composition in the Late Twentieth Century* (New York, Knopf, 1983)

Schaefer, J. *New Sounds: A Listener's Guide to New Music* (New York, Harper & Row, 1987)

Schwarz, K. R. 'Process vs. Intuition in the Recent Works of Steve Reich and John Adams', in *American Music* Vol. 8 No. 3, Autumn 1990

Schwarz, K. R. 'Steve Reich: Music as a Gradual Process', in *Perspectives of New Music* Vols. 19 and 20, 1980–1 and 1981–2

Strickland, E. *American Composers: Dialogues on Contemporary Music* (Bloomington, Indiana, Indiana University Press, 1991)

Strickland, E. *Minimalism: Origins* (Bloomington, Indiana, Indiana University Press, 1993)

Selective Discography

John Adams

The Chairman Dances
San Francisco Symphony conducted by Edo de Waart
NONESUCH 9 79144-2

The Death of Klinghoffer
Various performers, Orchestra of the Opera de Lyon
conducted by Kent Nagano
NONESUCH 9 79281-2 (2 CDs)

Fearful Symmetries
The Wound Dresser
Sanford Sylvan (baritone), Orchestra of St. Luke's
conducted by John Adams
NONESUCH 9 79218-2

Grand Pianola Music
Chamber Symphony
London Sinfonietta conducted by John Adams
NONESUCH 9 79219-2

Harmonielehre
San Francisco Symphony conducted by Edo de Waart
NONESUCH 9 79115-2

Harmonium
San Francisco Symphony Orchestra and Chorus
conducted by Edo de Waart
ECM NEW SERIES 1277

Nixon in China
Various performers, Orchestra of St. Luke's conducted
by Edo de Waart
NONESUCH 9 79177-2 (3 CDs)

Phrygian Gates
Shaker Loops
Mack McCray (piano), The Ridge Quartet
1750-ARCH RECORDS S-1784 (out of print)

Shaker Loops
San Francisco Symphony Orchestra conducted by Edo
de Waart; with Steve Reich's *Variations*
PHILIPS 412 214-2

Louis Andriessen

De Staat
Schönberg Ensemble conducted by Reinbert de Leeuw
NONESUCH 9 79251-2

De Stijl
M is for Man, Music, Mozart
Schönberg Ensemble conducted by Reinbert de Leeuw,
Astrid Seriese (voice), Orkest de Volharding conducted
by Jurjen Hempel
NONESUCH 9 79342-2

De Tijd
Schönberg Ensemble conducted by Reinbert de Leeuw
NONESUCH 9 79291-2

Philip Glass

Akhnaten
Various performers, Stuttgart State Opera Orchestra
and Chorus conducted by Dennis Russell Davies
CBS/SONY M2K 42457 (2 CDs)

La Belle et la Bête
Various performers, Philip Glass Ensemble conducted
by Michael Reisman
NONESUCH 79347-2 (2 CDs)

Einstein on the Beach
Philip Glass Ensemble conducted by Michael Riesman
NONESUCH 9 79323-2 (3 CDs)

Hydrogen Jukebox
Various performers, Philip Glass (piano), Allen
Ginsberg (narrator) conducted by Martin Goldray
NONESUCH 9 79286-2

Itaipu
The Canyon
Atlanta Symphony Orchestra and Chorus conducted
by Robert Shaw
SONY CLASSICAL SK 46352

Koyaanisqatsi
Various performers conducted by Michael Riesman
ANTILLES ASTA 1

'Low' Symphony
Brooklyn Philharmonic Orchestra conducted by
Dennis Russell Davies,
PHILIPS/POINT MUSIC 438 150-2

Music in Twelve Parts
Philip Glass Ensemble
VIRGIN 91311-2 (2 CDs)

Music with Changing Parts
Philip Glass Ensemble
NONESUCH 9 79325-2

Satyagraha
Various performers, The New York City Opera,
Orchestra and Chorus conducted by Christopher
Keene
CBS/SONY M3K 39672 (3 CDs)

Songs from Liquid Days
Various performers, Philip Glass Ensemble
CBS/SONY MK 39564

String Quartets Nos. 2–5
Kronos Quartet
NONESUCH 79356-2

Two Pages
Contrary Motion
Music in Fifths
Music in Similar Motion
Philip Glass Ensemble
NONESUCH 9 79326-2

Meredith Monk

Atlas
Various performers conducted by Wayne Hankin
ECM NEW SERIES 1491/92 (2 CDs)

Book of Days
Meredith Monk and Vocal Ensemble
ECM NEW SERIES 1399

Dolmen Music
Meredith Monk, various other performers
ECM NEW SERIES 1197

Turtle Dreams
Meredith Monk, various other performers
ECM NEW SERIES 1240

Michael Nyman

The Essential Michael Nyman Band
Michael Nyman Band
ARGO 436 820-2

Michael Nyman Songbook
Ute Lemper and the Michael Nyman Band
DECCA 425 227-2

The Piano
Michael Nyman (piano), members of the Munich
Philharmonic Orchestra conducted by Michael Nyman
VIRGIN CDVE 919

String Quartets Nos. 1–3
Balanescu Quartet
ARGO 433 093-2

The Man Who Mistook His Wife for a Hat
Various performers conducted by Michael Nyman
CBS/SONY MK 44669

Time Will Pronounce
Various performers
ARGO 440 282-2

Arvo Pärt

Arbos
The Hilliard Ensemble, Gidon Kremer (violin), Brass
Ensemble Staatsorchester Stuttgart conducted by
Dennis Russell Davies
ECM NEW SERIES 1325

Miserere
The Hilliard Ensemble, Orchester der Beethovenhalle
Bonn conducted by Dennis Russell Davies
ECM NEW SERIES 1430

Passio
The Hilliard Ensemble
ECM NEW SERIES 1370

Symphonies Nos. 1–3
Pro Et Contra
Perpetuum Mobile
Frans Helmerson (cello), Bamberg Symphony
Orchestra conducted by Neeme Järvi
BIS CD-434

Tabula Rasa
Gidon Kremer and Tatiana Gridenko (violins),
Lithuanian Chamber Orchestra conducted by Saulus
Sondeckis, various other performers
ECM NEW SERIES 1275

Te Deum
Estonian Philharmonic Chamber Choir, Tallinn
Chamber Orchestra conducted by Tõnu Kaljuste
ECM NEW SERIES 1505

Steve Reich

The Cave
Various performers, Steve Reich Ensemble conducted
by Paul Hillier
NONESUCH 79327-2 (2 CDs)

The Desert Music
Brooklyn Philharmonic, Steve Reich and Musicians
conducted by Michael Tilson Thomas
NONESUCH 9 79101-2

Different Trains
Electric Counterpoint
Kronos Quartet, Pat Metheny (guitar)
NONESUCH 9 79176-2

Drumming
Steve Reich and Musicians
NONESUCH 9 79170-2

Come Out
Piano Phase
Clapping Music
It's Gonna Rain
Double Edge: Nurit Tilles and Edmund Niemann
(pianos), Russ Hartenberger and Steve Reich
(clapping)
NONESUCH 9 79169-2

The Four Sections
Music for Mallet Instruments, Voices and Organ
London Symphony Orchestra conducted by Michael
Tilson Thomas, Steve Reich and Musicians
NONESUCH 9 79220-2

Music for 18 Musicians
Steve Reich and Musicians
ECM NEW SERIES 1129

Octet
Music for a Large Ensemble
Violin Phase
Steve Reich and Musicians
ECM New Series 1168

Sextet
Six Marimbas
Steve Reich and Musicians
Nonesuch 9 79138-2

Tehillim
Three Movements
Schönberg Ensemble with Percussion Group, The
Hague, conducted by Reinbert de Leeuw, London
Symphony Orchestra conducted by Michael Tilson
Thomas
Nonesuch 9 79295-2

Variations for Winds, Strings and Keyboards
San Francisco Symphony conducted by Edo de Waart;
with John Adams's *Shaker Loops*
Philips 412 214-2

Terry Riley

In C
Center of the Creative and Performing Arts in the State
University of New York at Buffalo led by Terry Riley
CBS/Sony MK 7178

A Rainbow in Curved Air
Poppy Nogood and the Phantom Band.
Terry Riley (all instruments)
CBS/Sony MK 7315

Salome Dances for Peace
Kronos Quartet
Nonesuch 9 79217-2 (2 CDs)

La Monte Young

Just Stompin'
The Forever Bad Blues Band
Gramavision R2 79487 (2 CDs)

The Second Dream of the High-Tension Line Stepdown
    Transformer
The Theatre of Eternal Music Brass Ensemble led by
Ben Neill
Gramavision R2 79467

The Well-Tuned Piano
La Monte Young (piano)
Gramavision R2 79452 (5 CDs)

Index

Page numbers in italics refer to
picture captions

Photographic Acknowledgements

Photographs by Joanne Akalaitis: 107, 112

Courtesy Boosey & Hawkes: photographs by Alix Jeffry 49, 74, 79; photographs by Malyse Albert 98; photograph by Dido Satman 100; photograph by Andrew Pothecary 102; photograph by Herning Lohner 105t; photograph by Michael McLaughlin 105b; photograph by James Poke 193; photograph by Camilla van Zuylen 204

Photograph by Tom Caravaglia: 132–3

Photograph by Carolyn Cassidy: 55

Cinematheque: 121

Courtesy ECM: photographs by Larry Watson 191, 214

Courtesy Elektra Nonesuch: photograph by Yannis Samaras 167; photographs by Richard Morganstein 180–1

Photograph by Betty Friedman: 134

Photographs by Gianfranco Gorgoni: 67, 69l

Photograph by Horst Huber: 140–1

The Hulton Deutsch Collection: 51, 53, 73, 82, 85, 95, 110, 118, 150, 163, 173

© Jasper Johns: 35

The Kobal Collection: Institute for Regional Education 152–3; André Paulvé Productions 162; BFI/United Artists 198–9; Jan Chapman Productions/Ciby 2000 202

Mason-Relkin Co.: 115

Performing Arts Library: photographs by Clive Barda 129, 145, 146, 148t, 148b, 169, 171

Photograph by Fred Plaut: 113

Corbis-Bettman: 20, 47, 52, 56, 59, 65, 68, 69t, 136, 158, 178, 185

Redferns: photograph by William Gottlieb 26; photograph by Steve Gillett 165; photograph by Christine Henderson 188; photographs by Malcolm Crowthers 195, 213

Rex Features: 38, 62

Courtesy Terry Riley: 25; photographs by Bob Benson 45, 46

© Ben Shahn: 90

Courtesy Gilbert and Lila Silverman Fluxus Collection Foundation: 7; photograph by George Maciunas 15

Courtesy Swatch: 108

Tate Gallery London/Bridgeman Art Library: 209

Courtesy Mary Jane Walsh Productions: 77, 94

© Robert Wilson: 131

Courtesy La Monte Young and Marian Zazeela: 18, 22, 32, 33; photograph by René Block 8; photograph by Marian Zazeela 17; photograph by Robert Adler 40–1; photograph by David Crossley 42